STACIE

MW00886567

Infinite Healing™

Empowering You to HEAL the Negative
So the Positive Can Flow Naturally!

МАНИЯ

Infinite Healing™

Empowering You to HEAL the Negative
So the Positive Can Flow Naturally!

STACIE FARNHAM

BALBOA.
PRESS

A DIVISION OF HAY HOUSE

Copyright © 2015 Stacie Farnham.

All rights reserved. No part of this book may be used or reproduced by any means, graphic, electronic, or mechanical, including photocopying, recording, taping or by any information storage retrieval system without the written permission of the publisher except in the case of brief quotations embodied in critical articles and reviews.

Balboa Press books may be ordered through booksellers or by contacting:

Balboa Press
A Division of Hay House
1663 Liberty Drive
Bloomington, IN 47403
www.balboapress.com
1 (877) 407-4847

Because of the dynamic nature of the Internet, any web addresses or links contained in this book may have changed since publication and may no longer be valid. The views expressed in this work are solely those of the author and do not necessarily reflect the views of the publisher, and the publisher hereby disclaims any responsibility for them.

The author of this book does not dispense medical advice or prescribe the use of any technique as a form of treatment for physical, emotional, or medical problems without the advice of a physician, either directly or indirectly. The intent of the author is only to offer information of a general nature to help you in your quest for emotional and spiritual well-being. In the event you use any of the information in this book for yourself, which is your constitutional right, the author and the publisher assume no responsibility for your actions.

Printed in the United States of America.

ISBN: 978-1-5043-2694-0 (sc)
ISBN: 978-1-5043-2696-4 (hc)
ISBN: 978-1-5043-2695-7 (e)

Library of Congress Control Number: 2015901219

Balboa Press rev. date: 02/04/2015

Contents

This book is dedicated to all of you who have tried so hard to be positive and still struggle; who have tried and not been able to let it go, get over it, forget about it, move on, come to terms with it, be the bigger person, forgive, or fake it 'til you make it; who seem to be continuously trying to let the same things go, get over the same event, forgive the same people, or pretend you don't feel "that" way; and finally, for those who are ready for a fresh perspective on HEALING. Maybe this is the answer you've been waiting for.

INTRODUCTION

Infinite Healing™ is an amazing HEALING technique that always takes *all* of YOU into consideration—Spirit, Mind, Heart, and Body. It will help you understand that everything that appears in your life is either a blessing or an opportunity to learn spiritual lessons and to HEAL, and it gives you the tools to be able to learn those lessons and to TRULY HEAL.

"HEALING" in Infinite Healing™ terms means something much deeper than other references to healing. It means to restore to perfect health—Spirit, Mind, Heart, and Body, to make whole, *as if nothing had happened*. Infinite Healing™ is about HONORING *every* part of YOU. It is about HONORING every symptom and HEALING at the Source. It is about HONORING every thought and HEALING at the Source, and it is about HONORING every emotion (past and present) and HEALING at the Source. It is about becoming aware of and HONORING who you are now and HEALING the things you don't like. It is about HONORING your past and HEALING the trauma you have carried with you. It is about TRULY HEALING, at infinite levels—Spirit, Mind, Heart, and Body—**at the Source**, at your Infinite Existence™.

Infinite Healing™ is not about treating symptoms, it is not about remedying causes, it is not about curing anything, it is not about clearing or releasing emotions, nor is it about suppressing, denying, or ignoring who you are, what you think, what you feel, or who you are.

Infinite Healing™ offers a new perspective on HEALING in that it empowers you to HONOR the negative and gives you the tools to TRULY HEAL the undesirable things in your life so the positive can flow naturally. It is important for you to understand that it is not focusing on the negative—it is **HONORING** the negative and **HEALING** the negative because ignoring or denying it does not mean it is not there. It is accepting that you're human and that your thoughts are not always pure and your emotions are not always positive, and it gives you the tools to HEAL undesirable thoughts and emotions.

It empowers you to become aware of what you're doing that is attracting what you don't want and gives you tools to HEAL those things so you can attract what you *do* want. If you want to encounter honest people in your life, you must HEAL the reason you're attracting dishonesty. If you want to experience respect, you must HEAL the reason you're experiencing disrespect, and if you want financial abundance, you must HEAL the reason you're not already financially abundant.

Infinite Healing™ is very personal. It is based on *your* perspective, *your* thoughts, *your* emotions, *your* beliefs, *your* experiences, and *your* life. It is dependent upon your willingness to be honest with yourself about what *you* perceive, what *you* think, what *you* feel, and what *you* believe. Infinite Healing™ is about *you* and requires you to become an active participant in your HEALING!

Within Infinite Healing™, many of the mentions of GOD and the Universe mean one and the same. GOD is the Universe, and the Universe is GOD. Both are referring to the higher power. We encourage you to use whichever word resonates with you.

As you read through this book you may become aware of things that you want or need to HEAL. I encourage you to use the NOTES pages at the end of the book to write them down *as they come to you* because you might not remember them later.

Note that when I reference high-level or higher-level energy, thoughts, and emotions, I am referring to positive energy, thoughts, and emotions; when I say low-level or lower-level, I am referring to negative energy, thoughts, and emotions.

UNCONDITIONAL LOVE & UNCONDITIONAL GRATITUDE™

Unconditional Love & Unconditional Gratitude™ is the divine Light of GOD, the Universe and is the foundation of Infinite Healing™.

"Unconditional" means without judgment, without conditions, without limits, regardless, total.

"Unconditional LOVE" means giving total and complete love without conditions. It means loving every person all the time, regardless of their opinions, their actions, their beliefs, etc. It means being loving in *every* situation—**no matter what!**

> *Where there is judgment,*
> *there is never Unconditional* LOVE.
> *Where there is fear,*
> *there is never Unconditional* LOVE.

"Unconditional Gratitude" means being grateful for every opportunity, for every experience, for every encounter, and appreciating all things in life. It is being grateful in *every* situation— **no matter what!**

When Unconditional Love is united with Unconditional Gratitude, you get Unconditional Love & Unconditional Gratitude™, which *is* the ultimate emotion for someone to experience. Unconditional Love & Unconditional Gratitude™ means that for *every* experience, you have no judgment, only Love. It means that for every person you encounter, you experience no judgment, only Love. Unconditional Love & Unconditional Gratitude™ means that for *every* experience, you are TRULY GRATEFUL, and it means that for *every* person you encounter, you are TRULY GRATEFUL.

Unconditional Love & Unconditional Gratitude™ is the ultimate objective. It frees you from the past, allows you to enjoy your NOW, and creates an abundant future. It allows you to TRULY enjoy life. Unconditional Love & Unconditional Gratitude™ removes limits and conditions, and it allows your life to flow in HARMONY.

Unconditional Love & Unconditional Gratitude™

THE INFINITE HEALING™ TOOLS

Helping you sweeten the "lemons" in life.

Infinite Healing™ follows ten basic principles and includes six main tools. The Infinite Healing™ tools and the Infinite Healing™ principles complement one another and are interconnected. It is helpful to understand the tools to apply as you go through the principles, yet it is important to understand the principles as you apply the tools. Therefore, I will explain the six main Infinite Healing™ tools, detail the ten Infinite Healing™ principles, and conclude with additional tools for you to use. Note that some concepts may be introduced in the tools and explained in further detail in the principles.

Infinite Healing™ Main Tools
1. **HONOR** yourself
2. **ACTIVATE** all lessons
3. **TRANSFORM** all Sources to
Unconditional Love &
Unconditional Gratitude™
4. **NAVIGATE** your life
5. **TRUST** that the outcome
will be exactly as it is supposed to be
6. Be **TRULY GRATEFUL**

<u>*Infinite Healing™ Principles*</u>
1. Everything is Energy
2. Everything is Influenced by Energy
3. You Exist at Infinite Levels
4. You Must HEAL at Infinite Levels to TRULY HEAL
5. Energy Follows Thought
6. What Your Mind Believes Creates Your Reality
7. Life is NOT Personal
8. You Attract What You Live
9. It IS What It IS
10. You Must HONOR You to TRULY HEAL

Everything you experience in life that triggers negative thoughts or emotions, whether you're an active participant or an observer, presents you with opportunities to HEAL. When you view all situations as opportunities to HEAL, you understand that life happens *for* YOU rather than *to* you. When you use the Infinite Healing™ tools, you'll HEAL spiritually, mentally, emotionally and physically. You will HEAL your past, your present, and your future. You will transform yourself, those around you, and the world. You *will* HEAL your life!

Use the six primary tools to use as often as possible when life gives you opportunities to HEAL.

INFINITE HEALING™ TOOL #1: HONOR YOURSELF

"To thine own self be true." —William Shakespeare

HONORING yourself is the most critical tool. When you're TRUE to yourself, you HONOR yourself. When you HONOR yourself, you become aware of what you think and what you feel, which makes you aware of many opportunities to HEAL. If you're not aware that there is an opportunity to HEAL, you cannot take advantage of the opportunity. If you do not HONOR yourself, it means that you deny, suppress, or ignore YOU, and you'll miss out on many opportunities to HEAL.

HONORING yourself means that you HONOR everything about you, that you allow every thought and you become aware of every emotion, that you recognize judgments, opinions, and beliefs. I know this can seem a bit alarming, but I assure you that as you continue through the tools, you'll learn how to HEAL the thoughts and emotions you have tried so hard to ignore and get rid of.

Infinite Healing™ HONORS everything about who you are now
so you can become aware of what you need to HEAL and
the TRUE YOU can be revealed.

Sometimes the turning point to HEALING is simply acknowledging that you think what you think and you feel what you feel and it is okay.

Negative thoughts and emotions
are how you know when
there are divine opportunities to HEAL!

Most importantly, when you HONOR yourself, you become aware of YOU! HONOR yourself and become aware of ... your thoughts, your emotions, your perceptions, your judgments, your beliefs, your symptoms, your limitations, your past, your present, and your future.

A great way to become aware of what you think is just to start writing or typing, unfiltered. Write what you think and what you feel about everything that comes to mind. This is a great way to HONOR YOU!

Infinite Healing™ *is an AWARENESS—of your thoughts, of your feelings, of your beliefs, of your life, of You. It is becoming aware of the negative thoughts that sabotage your life, whether those thoughts are yours or not, of the beliefs that interfere with you living in abundance, and of how you instinctively perceive life. It is becoming aware of the emotions that you instinctively feel in certain situations, and of the limitations that you have set for yourself or that you have accepted from others. It is an awareness of what you're living, what you're attracting, what you're creating, and most importantly, it is an awareness of You.*

Once you HONOR yourself and become aware that there is a divine opportunity to HEAL the next tool is to ACTIVATE all lessons.

INFINITE HEALING™ TOOL #2: ACTIVATE ALL LESSONS

One of the primary reasons for our life on earth is to grow spiritually, and one of the ways we do this is by learning lessons. I am not referring to lower-level lessons such as learning not to trust people because we were betrayed by someone or learning not to fully open ourselves up to love because we were in a relationship where we got hurt. The lessons we are here to learn are *never, ever* lower-level lessons. The lessons we are here to learn are *always* to be learned at the spiritual level. When we learn lessons at the spiritual level, we advance our Spirit. When we learn lessons at the spiritual level, it takes us closer to that ultimate objective of being able to live in Unconditional Love & Unconditional Gratitude™.

Lessons do not always have to be conscious. In fact, learning at the spiritual level means that many lessons are *not* conscious. Needing to know the lessons consciously puts you in the way of TRUE HEALING. Needing to have proof that you learned the lessons puts you in the way of TRUE HEALING. You do not have to know how you know— just TRUST that your Spirit knows.

Lessons do not always have to be complicated or profound. Sometimes the lesson might simply be to look at the situation from a different perspective, from a place where other people's actions are not about you, from a place where nothing is taken personally, from a place without judgment or from a place of Unconditional Love & Unconditional Gratitude™. Sometimes the lessons might be as simple as TRUSTING that GOD, the Universe, knows what is best *for* You.

This tool is also very important because if you have an opportunity to learn and you deny or ignore the opportunity, you *will* get another chance to learn those lessons, and another, and another, and yes, even another. Often, the later opportunities are much more blatant.

I have experienced this concept myself. I had been working on Infinite Healing™ for several years, keeping a notebook of ideas that came to me that I would eventually consolidate into a book. In my busy life of seeing clients, teaching students, and being a wife, a mother, a daughter, a sister, and a friend, the days went by. I would get a nudge every once in a while that I was to be working on Infinite Healing™, and I would think, "I know." Nudges would occur off and on throughout the years, but I honestly could not figure out how I could add one more thing to my life, even though I *knew* deep within my Heart what my priority was supposed to be. Well, apparently I said "I know" one too many times without taking action, and the next opportunity was more than a nudge. It was a full-on shove!

I play softball with my husband on a co-ed team, and one beautiful summer evening, I finally got the message loud and clear. I was running to home plate, and the ball happened to arrive ahead of me. Now, keep in Mind that although we used to play competitively many years ago, I took about ten years off while our daughters were growing up. Now that they were older, I decided to come out of "retirement" and play again. In the old days, sliding would have been second nature. But since I had just started playing again a couple of years prior, I no longer had confidence in my sliding abilities. So, here I was, running to home plate, and there was the catcher holding the ball. For some crazy reason, I heard in my Mind "slide!" So I attempted to slide. (I don't think it was a very graceful slide but I like to think it was just like the old days.) I think I blacked out for bit because the next thing I know I am laying at home plate and there were a lot of people around me. I looked at my left ankle and it was not pointing in a natural direction. What immediately went through my Mind was, "Infinite Healing." The x-rays confirmed that it was a complete break on the inside and outside ankle bones.

The experience was actually not very traumatic at all. I *knew* in my Heart what it was about, and I now had the time to consolidate everything I had written in notebooks over the last several years into what would eventually become much of this book. And for that I am infinitely GRATEFUL. I now try much harder to listen when I get those nudges because I know what pushing them aside can do.

Opportunity to learn lessons =
Opportunity to HEAL

You do not learn spiritual lessons when someone else fixes your problems, which means you'll get another chance. If you fix others' problems, you're denying or ignoring that they have an opportunity to learn. Helping others learn the lessons they are to learn and helping them HEAL is a much better option than trying to fix their problems and keeping the peace.

When you use the Infinite Healing™ tools,
you help GOD *and the Universe help You.*

Because you're part of the Universe and the Universe is part of you, you have everything you spiritually need *within* you. Because you have everything *within* you, it is easier than you might think to learn lessons at a spiritual level. You simply need to activate what you need from within. You do this by merely stating, verbally or silently: *"I activate all lessons that everyone is to learn from this experience."*
Don't think it's that easy? What if it *is?*
Experiences that trigger negative thoughts and emotions within you and others provide opportunities for multiple people to learn spiritual lessons. So, when you encounter people where your perception triggers negative emotions, not only do *you* have lessons to learn, but every other person who was involved in or witnessed the encounter has lessons to learn. If you tell other people about your experience and it triggers lower-level emotions for them, they also have lessons to learn. That is why we **activate all lessons that everyone is to learn from the experience**. Let's help others learn spiritual lessons with any opportunity we have because we will make this world a better place faster by doing so.
Sometimes in HEALING, especially if it is from a very traumatic experience, the HEALING has to be about YOU! In this case, you **activate all lessons that *I am* to learn from this experience.**

Eventually, you may be able to include everyone else, but if you feel drawn to make it personal, do so.

When dealing with difficult people, *activate all lessons*:

**"I activate all lessons that everyone is to learn
from encountering this person."**

In an accident (whether you're directly involved, witnessing it, or hearing about it), *activate all lessons*.

**"I activate all lessons that everyone is
to learn from this situation."**

In times of chaos or crisis, *activate all lessons*.

**"I activate all lessons that everyone is to
learn from this experience."**

Before you go to sleep, *activate all lessons*.

**"I activate all lessons that everyone is to
learn from today's experiences."**

Activate all lessons that everyone is to learn…

From current situations
From past situations
From others' situations

If you skip this tool, you may be denying or ignoring the opportunity to learn lessons, and you may very well get more opportunities.

> *Infinite Healing*™
> *helps* GOD, *the Universe*
> *help* YOU *learn*
> *your spiritual lessons and to* HEAL.

When you activate all lessons that everyone is to learn from an experience, they will either learn the spiritual lesson or they won't. Either way, it is certainly worth a try, and it definitely can't hurt.

Once you HONOR yourself and become aware that there is a divine opportunity to HEAL and you ACTIVATE all lessons, the next tool is to TRANSFORM all Sources to Unconditional Love & Unconditional Gratitude™.

INFINITE HEALING™ TOOL #3: TRANSFORM ALL SOURCES TO UNCONDITIONAL LOVE & UNCONDITIONAL GRATITUDE™

This tool is by far the most powerful, and in combination with Tool #2 (Activate all lessons), this is where TRUE HEALING takes place. The power behind this tool is that you actually transform (change) the energy of negative thought patterns (Sources) that trigger the negative emotions that create dis-ease* in not only your physical Body, but in your life, to the ultimate vibration of Unconditional Love & Unconditional Gratitude™.

> *Dis-ease is hyphenated throughout this book because I view all disturbances in the physical as a disruption or dis-ease in the energy flow rather than simply a deterioration of the Body.

There is a major difference between just love and gratitude and **Unconditional Love & Unconditional Gratitude**™; and between unconditional love and gratitude and **Unconditional Love & Unconditional Gratitude**™. Therefore, it is very important when using this tool that you're referencing **Unconditional Love & Unconditional Gratitude**™. Although it may seem like a lot to say, know that it can go through your Mind much faster than it can come out of your mouth. If it is easier for you, you may use UL & UG in lieu of Unconditional Love & Unconditional Gratitude™, but be careful not to cut your HEALING short by thinking it is too much to say. I use UL & UG when I write HEALING statements, but never when I am saying them.

You do not choose your emotions. Your emotions are *triggered* by your thoughts, which I will cover in greater detail in the Infinite Healing™ Principles. You instinctively feel how you feel based on your perception (thoughts) of a situation. You may be able to focus your attention on other emotions, but you do not choose how you feel in any given situation. Because your thoughts are the Sources of your emotions, it is very important to HEAL your thoughts. HEALING your thoughts immediately HEALS your emotions.

That is why in Infinite Healing™, we transform (change) all Sources (thoughts) of everything you're feeling to the absolute highest vibration of Unconditional Love & Unconditional Gratitude™.

This does not mean that once you transform all Sources of what you're feeling, you'll immediately feel Unconditional LOVE toward a person or be Unconditionally GRATEFUL for the experience. It means that you're changing the energy (of the negative thoughts that are triggering lower-level emotions) to a higher level. It means that you're HEALING the thoughts that trigger the negative emotions. It means that you'll have less negativity within you.

For example, when you transform all Sources of disappointment to Unconditional Love & Unconditional Gratitude™, you change the energy of the thought that triggered disappointment to a higher vibration, which HEALS both the thought and the emotion of disappointment. If you do not HEAL the thought that triggered the disappointment, it will be triggered again the next time you think about that situation.

When you transform all Sources of lower-level emotions to Unconditional Love & Unconditional Gratitude™, higher-level thoughts happen and positive emotions naturally follow. When you have more positive thoughts and higher-level emotions, you vibrate at a higher level. This means that you radiate *and* attract more positive energy.

Activating all lessons and
Transforming all Sources to
Unconditional Love &
Unconditional Gratitude™
= TRUE HEALING

When you transform all Sources, you HEAL all Sources, which HEALS your Spirit, your Mind, your Heart, and your Body, your past, your present, and your future, your consciousness, your subconsciousness, and your unconsciousness, every cell, every molecule, every atom, and everything in between, your Infinite Existence™, your life, the world, and the Universe.

Infinite Healing™ is TRUE HEALING at all levels—spiritually, mentally, emotionally, and physically. It is far beyond treating the symptom or remedying the cause. It is TRULY HEALING at the Source.

I encourage you to get away from concepts like releasing, letting it go, clearing, getting over it, forgetting about it, moving on, forcing positive thinking, coming to terms with it, being the bigger person, forgiving, making excuses, justifying, canceling, suppressing, denying, ignoring, and stuffing.

Although these may appear to be beneficial for you, they are all just forms of masking the symptom, like putting a patch over a hole in a piece of clothing. The patch may make the clothing functional and appear to be repaired, but the hole is still there. Negative thoughts and emotions create "holes" in your Spirit.

Another analogy is like cleaning house. What if every time you had garbage in your house, instead of taking it out to the trash receptacle, you stuffed it inside a closet? Once it is put in the closet and you close the door, you forget about it. You may notice it the next time you go to hide garbage, but it is easy to ignore or pretend that it is not there, and you just keep filling the closet. If that one gets full, you stuff it in a different one. You may have signs that the trash is rotting, but you can hide the awful odor with air freshener, open the windows to air out the house, wear nose plugs so you cannot smell, or you just deal with it and learn to ignore the awful aroma. No matter what you do to avoid actually cleaning your house, if you do not get rid of the trash, everything else is just hiding what is really going on, and the contents of the closets continue to decay. Your negative thoughts and emotions are the garbage, and the closets are parts of your physical Body. When you do not HONOR and HEAL your "garbage" and you "hide" it away, it does not mean that it is no longer there. It *will* begin to decay and break you down—spiritually, mentally, emotionally, and physically.

If you were to take a glass and throw it on the floor, it would break into many pieces. Now say "I'm sorry." The glass is not miraculously put back together. It is still in pieces on the floor. Even though the glass may have forgiven you for throwing it on the floor, it is still broken into pieces. Saying or hearing "I'm sorry" does not HEAL what is felt. Forgiving does not HEAL the hurt or pain. Pretending that it didn't happen does not HEAL.

Just because you do not HONOR your thoughts and emotions, or are not aware of what you think and feel, does not mean that the negative is not there. Convincing yourself that you shouldn't think or feel that way does not mean it has gone away. Moving on, getting over it, or being the bigger person does not mean you were not hurt, disappointed, or angry. Whichever example above you want to use, you can see that if you do not TRULY HEAL the negative things in your life, you're just ignoring that the negative is there.

Releasing, letting go of, and clearing are all simply a *transfer* of energy where the negative emotion you do not want is transferred from you to somewhere outside of you. For example, you release, let go of, or clear anger. The energy of anger is transferred from within you to somewhere outside of you, and is now in the Universe for you to pick up again or for someone or something else to pick up (your family, your pet, or your friends).

Since there is *never* a space with *no* energy, when you release, let go of, or clear energy (transfer), "another" energy will immediately take its place. You do not know what energy fills the void, so make sure that you replace it with something great like Unconditional Love & Unconditional Gratitude™. However, understand that replacing takes that "something great" from somewhere else in the Universe.

Letting it go, getting over it, forgetting about it, moving on, coming to terms with it, being the bigger person, making excuses, or trying to justify it are all concepts of trying to convince yourself that you do not feel what you really feel or felt, or trying to ignore what you really feel or felt. It does not HEAL the emotion or why you feel or felt that way.

Forcing positive thinking is trying to convince yourself that you think something different than you actually think or striving to change the focus of your attention to something positive. Likewise, forcing positive feelings is attempting to convince yourself that you feel something different than you actually feel or trying to change the focus of your attention on a positive emotion. Neither of these HEALS the reason you think or feel the way you do.

The Merriam-Webster dictionary's definition of forgive is "to cease to feel resentment against (an offender)." Forgiving does not mean that what happened did not happen, and it does not mean that you do not still feel the emotions that were triggered by the event. Forgiving is sometimes saying, "I am willing to overlook what you have done *to* me." Forgiving comes from the viewpoint that life happens *to* you, based on the perspective that someone did something *to* you. The need to forgive is based on judgment, and where there is judgment, there is *never* Unconditional LOVE. Forgiveness does *not* HONOR YOU and it certainly does not HEAL the reason why you think or feel the way you do. That is why it can be so difficult, and why it still triggers the lower-level emotions when you think about the situation.

> **"Working on this forgiveness thing
> is a full-time job."** —*Unknown*

Cancelling puts energy in a neutral state. As you'll learn in detail later, it is your thoughts and emotions that give energy direction and strength. When you cancel energy and put it in a neutral state, it is then random thoughts and emotions that will attach to that energy. So, if you do cancel energy, remember to use the Infinite Healing™ tools to **activate all lessons** and **transform all Sources to Unconditional Love & Unconditional Gratitude™**.

To suppress is to bury what you really think or really feel. To deny is not to admit that you think what you think or feel the way you feel. To ignore is to pretend that you do not think what you think or feel the way you feel. All of these are just stuffing the negative deep inside. None of these HONOR what you really think and what you really feel, and none of these HEAL the reason you think or feel the way you do.

In all of the concepts mentioned above, the wound is still there, negatively affecting your Spirit, Mind, Heart, and Body. None of these HEAL your perspective, so when you think about the situation again, it can trigger the same lower-level emotions. None of these HEAL the way you feel, and none of these TRULY HEAL the trauma. Do you want to patch it, or do you want to HEAL it? Do you want to hide it away, or do you want to HEAL it? Although some of these concepts can be effective and help you feel better, transforming all Sources to Unconditional Love & Unconditional Gratitude™ is more effective because **transforming all Sources to Unconditional Love**

& Unconditional Gratitude™ HEALS the thoughts that trigger the lower-level emotions.

> *Infinite Healing*™ *is not*
> *forcing positive thoughts and emotions.*
> *It is* HEALING *the Sources of*
> *negative emotions as they arise rather than*
> *suppressing, denying, or ignoring them and*
> *allowing them to settle in the physical.*
> *It is* HEALING *the Sources of*
> *negative thoughts and emotions*
> *so the positive ones flow naturally.*

Transforming energy actually alters the energy from one form to another. For example, when you transform all Sources of anger to Unconditional Love & Unconditional Gratitude™, you change the energy of the thought that triggered the anger to Unconditional Love & Unconditional Gratitude™. Transforming all Sources to Unconditional Love & Unconditional Gratitude™ *is* HEALING.

Intent matters. Are you doing it to get rid of it, or are you doing it to HEAL? If you're transforming all Sources just to get the thought, the feeling, or the symptom to go away, it may be a form of suppressing, denying, or ignoring, and may not be as effective as if you're transforming all Sources to Unconditional Love & Unconditional Gratitude™ to TRULY HEAL in Spirit, Mind, Heart, and Body.

It is imperative that you HONOR your thoughts and HONOR your feelings. *That* is the first step in HEALING. However, know that you do not always need to know what all of the Sources are. Remember that the Universe knows all, and you *can* HEAL at infinite levels without everything being at the conscious level. Recognize that there is an opportunity to HEAL and then use the tools to do it! When an emotion is triggered by your perception of a situation, you're actually feeling several emotions at the same time. You do not need to know what all of those emotions are or why you're feeling them or why you think the way you do. You do not need to know why people do the things they do or why people are the way they are. Needing to know *why* gets you stuck in the limited human Mind, gets you trapped in logic, and stagnates the flow of energy. Needing to know *why* puts you in the way of your HEALING. HONOR and accept that you think the way you think, you feel the way you feel, and you are who you are. Then use the Infinite Healing™ tools to HEAL the things you do not want.

> *If you're not getting the results that you*
> *want or expect with Infinite Healing™,*
> *you're likely in the way.*
> HEALING *is only limited by YOU!*

To change your reality, you must HEAL the energy that is creating your current reality. Like a computer, the data is only as good as the information that is programmed or input. If programming is negative, the results or output has no alternative but to be negative. Even if you sometimes input positive data, the output will be negative because the computer has been programmed that way. When the programming is changed to a positive, the results or output *will* be positive (even with a little negative input).

Remember that transforming actually *changes* the vibration of the energy. When Sources are transformed into Unconditional Love & Unconditional Gratitude™, it changes the vibration of lower-level energy to the ultimate vibration of Unconditional Love & Unconditional Gratitude™. Transforming energy to Unconditional Love & Unconditional Gratitude™ puts more Unconditional Love & Unconditional Gratitude™ into the Universe—that is how transforming all Sources to Unconditional Love & Unconditional Gratitude™ transforms not only you, but those around you, and the world.

Infinite Healing™ *is*
a transformation of you, of those around you,
of the world, of the Universe.

When you HONOR everything about yourself and become aware that there is an opportunity to HEAL:

"I activate all lessons
that everyone is to learn from this experience.
I transform all Sources of everything I am feeling to
Unconditional Love & Unconditional Gratitude™**."**

The greatest HEALING occurs when you **HEAL it while you're in it.** Do not wait until later! In order to wait until later to HEAL, you must suppress, ignore, or deny what you're thinking and feeling *at that moment.* Waiting until later makes you miss the opportunity to HEAL at the deepest levels.

Sometimes you may need to step away to HEAL it while you're in it. That's okay! If you need to step away from the situation and take the time you need to HONOR what you think and HONOR what you feel, do so! At one of our family functions, negative emotions were triggered within me, and although I tried to HEAL it then, I wasn't feeling the results as quickly as I normally do. So I went to another room, activated all lessons that everyone was to learn from that experience and transformed all Sources of everything I was feeling to Unconditional Love & Unconditional Gratitude™. I felt myself HEALING and after several minutes was able to rejoin the family with a much more positive attitude. However, know that because you can do Infinite Healing™ in your Mind, it can be easy to HEAL it while you're in it in most cases without stepping away.

You often feel many emotions all at once and it may be impractical to try to define *all* of what you're feeling at any given moment. If you can identify some of what you're feeling, HEALING occurs at an even deeper level, but do not get caught up in trying to figure out what you're feeling. If you get stuck on trying to figure out what the feelings are, you get in the way. If you can identify what you feel, do so. If not, just do the HEALING. That is why you should always include "and everything else I am feeling." Also understand that sometimes you just can't put it into words what you are feeling. That is why sometimes I just HEAL "Aaaaaaahhhhhhhhh" or "all of this."

When you experience negative emotions, say:

**"I activate all lessons
that everyone is to learn from this experience.
I transform all Sources of anger,
frustration, disappointment,
and everything else I am feeling
to Unconditional Love & Unconditional Gratitude™."**

HEAL it while you're in it. Do not wait until later!

When you have a physical symptom:

**"I activate all lessons
that everyone is to learn from this condition.
I transform all Sources of this condition to
Unconditional Love & Unconditional Gratitude™."**

In the case of a headache:

**"I activate all lessons
that everyone is to learn from all experiences that have created
or contributed to this pain in my head.
I transform all Sources of everything I am feeling that
has created or contributed to the pain in my head to
Unconditional Love & Unconditional Gratitude™."**

HEAL it while you're in it. Do not wait until later!

*NOTE: In this example, we are referring to a headache. When it comes to physical symptoms, never own the negative. The Body part is yours—the symptom is not. Therefore, it is "**the** pain in **my** head" rather than "my headache." Never make negative energy yours. However, please note that if you have pain in your head and pain in your neck and you HEAL only the pain in your head, the pain in your neck may still be there.*

*ALSO NOTE: It is important that you do not transform the pain. Doing so may help the pain lessen or go away for a while, but because the physical Body follows your emotions that are triggered by your thoughts (you'll learn more about this in the Infinite Healing™ Principles), it is important to transform **all Sources** of everything that you're feeling that created the pain to Unconditional Love & Unconditional Gratitude™.*

You will HEAL deeper if you know the emotion that impacts the particular part of the Body in which you have discomfort. For example, dread and anxiety adversely affect and often store in the stomach.

In the case of symptoms in the stomach:

"I activate all lessons
that everyone is to learn from all experiences
that have created or contributed to the pain in my stomach. I
transform all Sources of dread, anxiety, and everything else I
am feeling to
Unconditional Love & Unconditional Gratitude™."

HEAL it while you're in it. Do not wait until later!

Find more information in the Physical Reference Chart at the back of the book.

When you become aware that you're judging yourself or someone else:

> **"I activate all lessons**
> **that everyone is to learn from this experience.**
> **I transform all Sources**
> **of judgment of myself and others to**
> **Unconditional Love & Unconditional Gratitude™."**

When you pass an accident, police car, fire truck, ambulance, or hear sirens:

> **"I activate all lessons**
> **that everyone is to learn from that situation.**
> **I transform all Sources of that situation to**
> **Unconditional Love & Unconditional Gratitude™."**

Those are first three main Infinite Healing™ tools for you to use most consistently to achieve the greatest and deepest HEALING.

1. **HONOR** YOURSELF
2. **ACTIVATE** ALL LESSONS
3. **TRANSFORM** ALL SOURCES TO UNCONDITIONAL LOVE & UNCONDITIONAL GRATITUDE™

The next three tools are to be used to help you attract what you want in life.

4. **NAVIGATE** YOUR LIFE
5. **TRUST** THAT THE OUTCOME WILL BE EXACTLY AS IT IS SUPPOSED TO BE
6. BE TRULY **GRATEFUL**

INFINITE HEALING™ TOOL #4: NAVIGATE YOUR LIFE

Navigating your life is telling GOD, the Universe what you want. It is like setting your GPS for a certain destination. This tool has two options: **set the energy the way you want it** or **activate all Sources that create what you want**. Both navigate your life the way you want it to be. You can use one or you can use both.

Setting the energy the way you want it is simply stating how you want things in your life to be. But understand that if you feel like you're lying to yourself as you set the energy you're not doing what you think you're doing. For example, if you set the energy that "I *am* financially abundant" but you doubt it, do not believe it, or know differently, you have negated the energy and you probably will not get the results you want.

Affirmations *are* setting the energy. Because energy follows thought (which I'll cover in detail later), **you set the energy with every thought**.

"I always ..."
"You're going to be late ..."
"I can't lose weight no matter what I do."
"I can't eat that because ..."
"Gas prices are going up."
"You never ..."
"We can't afford ..."
"I don't have any money."

You **set the energy with every thought** that goes through your Mind! Yet another reason for you to listen to your thoughts, and why HEALING at the Source is so important!

When setting the energy, make sure you're setting it to attract what you want! When you become aware that you have set the energy (had a thought) for something you didn't want, **transform all**

Sources of that potential to Unconditional Love & Unconditional Gratitude™. Then set the energy the way you DO want it.

When you activate all Sources that create what you want, you activate all thought patterns that will create what you want. This is not just *your* thought patterns, but *all* thought patterns. This is more action-based and is often more believable than just telling the Universe what you want and expecting to get it. Activating all Sources makes things seem possible.

"I activate all Sources that create *my* financial abundance."

vs.

"I *am* financially abundant."

For some, activating all Sources that create *my* financial abundance may seem more promising than stating that "I *am* financially abundant" when you may know, in your current reality, that it is *not* TRUE. In this case, you have already negated the affirmation by the doubt that it is TRUE or the knowing that you're not really financially abundant.

However, be cautious about telling the Universe what you want because the way energy works, you may very well get exactly what you asked for. For example, you have found a house that has "everything you want." You set the energy that this is your house. You put pictures of it on your vision board. You tell the Universe that it is what you want. However, unbeknownst to you, the house has electrical and structural problems that you also get when you get your "dream" house. Sometimes being very specific with what you want limits what you could have.

When you activate all Sources that create what you want or you set the energy the way you want it, one of two things will happen. Either you'll get what you want, or you won't. If you get what you want, be TRULY GRATEFUL (*Infinite Healing*™ *Tool #6*). If you don't, there are two primary reasons—either it was not in your best spiritual interest (at this time or ever), or you're in the way of getting what you want, and you still have some lessons to learn and HEALING to do.

Activating all Sources that create what you want and setting the energy the way you want it is living life *consciously* and is *navigating your life*. It is not leaving what happens in your life up to chance.

When you activate all Sources that create what you want or set the energy the way you want, it increases the direction of the energy for that potential to happen. If you don't navigate your life, that potential has the same possibility as any other potential.

The more often you're reminded to tell the Universe what you want, the more you reinforce the concept. Find something that reminds you to regularly tell the Universe what you want.

As an example, for financial abundance I use the Chevy Avalanche. To me, this represents my avalanche of money. Every time I see a Chevy Avalanche, I recite my financial abundance mantra of, "I activate all Sources that create *my* financial abundance." As I drive around town, I generally see many Avalanches, and each time it reminds me to activate all Sources that create what I want. But make sure not to limit yourself. For instance, I thought I saw a Chevy Avalanche heading toward me, so I started to state my financial abundance mantra but noticed as the vehicle got closer that it was not an Avalanche after all. I realized that I had stopped what I was saying and by doing so, had just limited myself. In that case, it was a Cadillac Escalade. So I now state my financial abundance mantra when I see a Chevy Avalanche, a Cadillac Escalade, a Honda Ridgeline, and oftentimes when I just see a Chevy, Cadillac, or Honda.

I personally find it most effective to activate all Sources that create what I want because to me, it feels like I am taking action, and it seems that the possibilities are higher rather than just telling the Universe what I want.

*Infinite Healing™ is a new perspective on the law of attraction and gives you the tools to HEAL what is attracting the things you do not want and teaching you how to attract the things you **do** want.*

When you activate all Sources that create a situation to flow in Unconditional Love & Unconditional Gratitude™, it sets it up for the best possible outcome for all involved.

Stop trying to control life. Stop trying to control the outcome of everything. Stop fearing that things might not turn out the way *you* think they should. Stop worrying about what *may* go wrong. Stop expecting things to be the way they've always been. Stop trying to force things to happen. Stop getting in the way of the flow of life.

When you try to control anything, *you get in the way.* Let go of the wheel of life and let the Universe drive. You are here as the navigator of your life, not the driver. Just like it creates a challenge if two people are trying to drive the same car in separate directions, it creates complications in your life when you and GOD are trying to drive your life in different directions. GOD can see *all* possibilities; you can only see as far as your experiences. Be cautioned that sometimes the Universe may just let you have the wheel and you could end up creating more challenges, thus providing you with many more opportunities to HEAL.

Sometimes the greatest gifts in life
are the ones you do not expect!

Navigate your life in the direction you would like it to go, and then TRUST that whatever appears in your life is always, always *for* You.

Infinite Healing™ Tool #5: TRUST that the Outcome Will be Exactly as it is Supposed to BE

Once you have navigated your life where you want it to go, have complete Trust that the outcome was, is, or will be exactly the way it is supposed to Be. If it could have been different, it would have been. If it was supposed to have been different, it would have been. Whatever outcome occurs in any experience, you either Trust in God, the Universe (life happens *for* You), or you're a victim of life (life happens *to* you). Remember that God can see *all* possibilities; you can only see as far as your experiences and what you're conscious of. Trust in the Universe, Trust in God, Trust that God, the Universe, always knows what is best *for* You. The bigger Plan is often difficult to understand, but it does not mean that there isn't one.

If you do not have complete Trust, you get in the way of attracting what you want. Get out of the way and let the energy work the way it needs to be *for* You, the way it is supposed to be *for* You. One of the most common things that you can do to get in the way and interfere with attracting what you want is by having an attachment to the outcome. Having an attachment to the outcome is when you want something to turn out a certain way or you want something not to turn out a certain way. When you're attached to the outcome of a situation, you attract what you fear the outcome will or won't be. Fear of it not turning out the way you want it or the way you think it should be can negate the energy you have set or get in the way of it happening. When you have an attachment to the outcome, you no longer live in complete Trust.

When you're attached to the outcome, it puts you in the way of life flowing in Unconditional Love & Unconditional Gratitude™.

If you have an issue with the word Trust, there are other words you can use here, one of which is Surrender. This is where you surrender your life to the higher power. If you have a negative perception of the word Surrender, you can use Faith. Have Faith that you're exactly where you're meant to be, and have Faith that God is always with you in whatever you're going through. Use whatever word resonates with You.

INFINITE HEALING™ TOOL #6: BE TRULY GRATEFUL

In our busy lives filled with daily responsibilities, we often take for granted or overlook the little gifts in life. The fact is that there are things to be TRULY GRATEFUL for throughout the day, *every* day. Our lives are divinely orchestrated and everything happens for a reason, whether we can make sense of it or not (and that reason is to learn spiritual lessons to advance our Spirit). Try to find something to be TRULY GRATEFUL for in *every* situation.

Do not pretend you are grateful for the things you "should" be grateful for, for the things society says you're to be grateful for. Be TRULY GRATEFUL for the things that make you *feel* grateful. TRUE GRATITUDE fills you up to where you feel like you just can't expand any further, where it is so encompassing that you feel like you're about to burst, where you smile just because.

If you can't be TRULY GRATEFUL for something, don't pretend that you are. You might have something that someone else doesn't, but that doesn't mean you're TRULY GRATEFUL for what you have. Know that GOD, the Universe, knows the difference between when you're TRULY GRATEFUL and when it is just words.

Remember that energy follows thought, so being TRULY GRATEFUL for the small things, attracts big things to be TRULY GRATEFUL for. It is difficult to be TRULY GRATEFUL when you're stuck in negative thoughts and lower-level emotions.

As you continue to TRULY HEAL, you'll experience TRUE GRATITUDE for the simplest things in life like each and every day, all levels of HEALING, no matter how minor, every time the energy works the way you want it, every person you encounter, every opportunity to learn a lesson, every sunrise and sunset, every smile, every gift, big or small, that is presented in your life. You can even be TRULY GRATEFUL for a red light or a missed plane, the beauty of nature, and even the simplest moments.

What makes YOU smile just because?

Those are the six main Infinite Healing™ tools. Remember that tools 1-3 are the ones you'll use most consistently to get the deepest levels of HEALING.

1. **HONOR** YOURSELF
2. **ACTIVATE** ALL LESSONS
3. **TRANSFORM** ALL SOURCES TO UNCONDITIONAL LOVE & UNCONDITIONAL GRATITUDE™

Tools 4-6 are for you to use to attract what you want.

4. **NAVIGATE** YOUR LIFE
5. **TRUST** THAT THE OUTCOME WILL BE EXACTLY AS IT IS SUPPOSED TO BE
6. BE TRULY **GRATEFUL**

You now have the tools to HEAL yourself—Spirit, Mind, Heart, and Body—and your life. The key now is to remember to use them, which may be a very conscious effort at first. As you begin your TRUE HEALING journey where you HONOR who you are now and become aware of what you really think and what you really feel, it may seem like you're **activating all lessons** and **transforming all Sources** all the time. It did for me. In fact, I thought I *was* a positive person until I began to pay attention to the thoughts that went through my Mind and the feelings that were triggered. But as I continued to HEAL the negative parts of me that I had ignored for so many years, I revealed something wonderful, which was a ME who can see the world and the people in it without judgment (most of the time), a ME who is TRULY GRATEFUL for so many things that I often smile just because, a ME who understands at a spiritual level what Unconditional LOVE is, and a ME who is unfiltered. I discovered the TRUE ME, and for that, I am infinitely TRULY GRATEFUL.

Use the Infinite Healing™ tools *every time* you experience:

Less-than-desirable thoughts
Less-than-desirable emotions
Less-than-desirable situations
Less-than-desirable people

The Infinite Healing™ tools—LEARN them, USE them, LIVE them, and create a life that flows in Unconditional Love & Unconditional Gratitude™.

**"I activate all Sources
that create me remembering to use the
Infinite Healing™ tools regularly
to TRULY HEAL me and my life."**
"I activate all Sources that create TRUE HEALING in ME!"

Infinite Healing™
gives you the tools to TRULY HEAL
*the things about yourself and in your life
that you do not like.*

THE INFINITE HEALING™ PRINCIPLES

Now that you have a basic understanding of how to apply the six main Infinite Healing™ tools, let's go over the Infinite Healing™ Principles.

Infinite Healing™ Principles
1. Everything is Energy
2. Everything is Influenced by Energy
3. You Exist at Infinite Levels
4. You Must HEAL at Infinite Levels to TRULY HEAL
5. Energy Follows Thought
6. What Your Mind Believes Creates Your Reality
7. Life is NOT Personal
8. You Attract What You Live
9. It IS What It IS
10. You Must HONOR YOU to TRULY HEAL

INFINITE HEALING™ PRINCIPLE #1: EVERYTHING IS ENERGY

Everything is energy, and *energy does not always make sense to the human Mind.* When you come to understand these two basic concepts, there will never be any limits to your life, and you'll realize that literally, **anything is possible!** A word of advice to those with analytical and over-analytical Minds—trying to put logic to the things you can do with energy *will* cause confusion and is often impossible.

In very simplistic terms, quantum physics states that the Universe is one single gigantic field of energy. This field includes *everything,* and *everything* is within this field, from matter (trees, computers, books, cars, water, animals, and people) to non-matter (thoughts, emotions, music, imagination, words, dreams, and prayer). This book is energy, the cell phone you use is energy, your physical Body is energy, your thoughts are energy, your emotions are energy, your kitchen table is energy, and your pet is energy. *Everything, without exception, is energy.*

The difference in energy is the rate at which it vibrates. This subject goes much deeper than we will discuss here, but understand that positive thoughts, emotions, and words have a high vibration while negative thoughts and emotions have a low vibration. Negative words, even spoken in jest, have a low vibration.

Energy is neutral and without reasoning capacity. It is our thoughts that give energy direction, and it is our feelings that give it power. *The vibration of the emotions always matches the vibration of the thoughts.* The stronger the emotion associated with the thought, the stronger the energy. Whatever you think about that has a strong emotion attached to it (fear, hate, Unconditional LOVE, Unconditional GRATITUDE) influences the energy within and around you *strongly and quickly.*

According to the first law of thermodynamics, energy can neither be created nor destroyed—it can only be transferred or transformed. To transfer energy means to take energy from one place and move it to another. To **transform** energy means to *change* the energy to a different vibration. Energy can *only* be changed by transforming or by entrainment, which we will discuss shortly.

There are many approaches to energy work that encourage releasing, letting go of, or clearing negative thoughts and emotions, which can be very powerful. However, with these approaches, energy is simply being transferred from within you to somewhere outside of you. As we used in an example before, if you're angry, you may release, let go of, or clear the anger from within you. Although that can be beneficial for you personally, it puts whatever you're releasing into the Universe, which in this case is anger. Any energy that is in the Universe is out there for you to pick up, for someone else to pick up (i.e. a loved one), or for some*thing* else to pick up (your furniture, car, computer, cell phone, radio, pet, etc.). Transferring energy is simply moving it from one place to another.

Transforming all Sources to
Unconditional Love &
Unconditional Gratitude™
puts more
Unconditional Love &
Unconditional Gratitude™
into the Universe.

Infinite Healing™
is divinely inspired to transform you,
transform those around you,
transform your life, transform the world,
and transform the Universe!

Often, when you learn a technique, it becomes habit until you consciously or deliberately change it. As you begin to use the Infinite Healing™ tools, make it a conscious effort to *transform all Sources to Unconditional Love & Unconditional Gratitude*™ rather than releasing, letting go of, clearing, cancelling, or anything else that may have become routine for you to do. There is a considerable difference, and Infinite Healing™ produces significantly different results.

INFINITE HEALING™ PRINCIPLE #2: EVERYTHING IS INFLUENCED BY ENERGY

Resonance is the rate at which energy vibrates—it is the rhythm of the energy. The vibration of your overall energy at any given moment matches the vibration of your thoughts and emotions. Whatever frequency you're vibrating at is the rate of the energy you radiate. When you have happy experiences and you feel happy, you radiate happiness. When you have not-so-happy experiences and you feel sad, you radiate sadness. You can generally tell whether people are happy or not-so-happy by watching them or interacting with them. If they are happy (vibrating at a high rhythm), they radiate happiness (high-level energy). If they are sad (vibrating at a low rhythm), they radiate sadness (low-level energy).

Entrainment is when two vibrations or rhythms match each other. In the case of a high vibration and a low vibration coming near each other, one of three things will happen. One, the low vibration will rise, which is the most common because positive energy always trumps negative energy. Two, the high vibration will lower, or three, both rhythms will change (high vibration lowers and low vibration rises).

One example of entrainment is the croaking of bullfrogs. During the evening, when the bullfrogs begin to croak, you'll hear them sporadically. Eventually, they all begin to croak together. Another example is lightning bugs. When they first begin to light, they each light at their own rhythm. Eventually, they all light at the same time. Grandfather clocks all lined up on a wall will eventually entrain to each other and all the pendulums will swing in unison. Menstrual cycles are another example of entrainment. Several women living in the same household will often end up on the same cycle because they are entraining to each other. *Note: when you're able to maintain your own vibration, you'll never entrain to someone else's cycle.*

So, entrainment occurs when two or more energies come near each other, and because there is *never* a space with *no* energy, energy is *always* coming in contact with other energy. When you vibrate and radiate positive energy, lower-level energy may entrain to a more positive vibration to try to match your vibration. When you're happy, the chances are high that you can make others happier.

Through entrainment, **the vibration of *your* energy continually affects other energy**, which in turn has an overall impact on the energy of the Universe. How's that for a good reason to HEAL yourself?

Just as the resonance of *your* energy affects other energy, the vibration of *other* energy can affect *your* energy. When you experience a frequency lower than yours, you may feel your energy decrease. When you experience a rhythm higher than yours (i.e. from a person happier than you are) you may feel your energy begin to rise. Being around a happy person will often make you feel happier, and being around a sad person will sometimes make you sad. The vibration of *other* energy can affect *your* energy and the energy that is in the Universe. Talk about incentive to help others HEAL.

Through resonance and entrainment, **your energy influences everything around you**. But know that resonance and entrainment does not only apply to people. Because *everything* is energy, it applies to *everything* around you—pets, appliances, plants, vehicles, computers, etc.

> *Because you radiate*
> *the vibration of your energy,*
> *your energy influences the world.*
> *Never underestimate the power of You!*

You not only radiate the frequency of your energy, but you also *attract* the same vibration as your energy. In other words, whatever energy you radiate *at any given moment* is the same level of energy that you attract. Positive energy radiates and attracts positive energy, and negative energy radiates and attracts negative energy.

When you're out of HARMONY in Spirit, Mind, Heart, or Body, you resonate at a negative, lower-level vibration. Then when you come in contact with lower-level energy, it is possible that your energy will entrain to an even lower level. Have you ever noticed that when one thing goes wrong, multiple things tend to go wrong? Chaos on the inside creates chaos on the outside. Chaos attracts chaos. Dis-HARMONY attracts dis-HARMONY. Judgment attracts judgment. Anger attracts anger, and sadness attracts sadness.

When you learn how to TRULY HEAL the lower-level thoughts and emotions and are in HARMONY with life, you vibrate at a positive, high-level frequency. Then, when you come in contact with lower-level energy, it is very likely that you'll entrain that energy to a higher level. When you're in HARMONY in Spirit, Mind, Heart, and Body, you'll radiate and attract positive, high-level energy. This means that your energy likely entrains other energy higher and you attract more high-level energy. Have you ever noticed that life seems to flow better when you're happy? Happiness attracts happiness, HARMONY attracts HARMONY, Unconditional Love & Unconditional Gratitude™ attracts Unconditional Love & Unconditional Gratitude™. When you're at a positive, high-level frequency, it is easier for you to maintain your own rhythm rather than your energy entraining to other energy. Remember when I said that *when you're able to maintain your own vibration, you'll never entrain to someone else's cycle?* This is what I meant.

Since energy can only be transferred or transformed, if you think you're picking up on others' negative energy, that means some of your energy must be being transferred out of you to allow this. Consider this alternative. What if you're *not* picking up on others' negative energy, but you're *entraining* to it? This means you have that same frequency of energy somewhere within you and you now have a prime opportunity to learn lessons and HEAL it! I personally used to be very sensitive to energy. I can still sense the energies around me, but they do not affect me like they used to. Knowing what I know now, I am certain I was entraining to the lower-level energies rather than actually picking up on other people's stuff. Now that I have HEALED so much of the negative within me, I am almost always able to maintain my own high vibration and am rarely affected by negative energies. When I am, I use the Infinite Healing™ tools to **activate all lessons** and **HEAL**.

Everything is influenced by energy. Your perception of a situation and the emotions that are triggered by your perception is the vibration of energy you radiate to that situation. In other words, what *you* think of a situation influences the frequency of the energy of *the* situation that you're observing or thinking about. If you observe an accident and perceive it as a traumatic event, you radiate trauma to the accident. If you observe an accident and feel sorry for the people involved, you radiate sorrow to the incident. If you observe an accident and **activate all lessons that everyone is to learn from that experience** and **transform all Sources of that situation to Unconditional Love & Unconditional Gratitude**™, you not only influence the energy of that situation in a positive way, but you also radiate Unconditional Love & Unconditional Gratitude™ to the accident and those involved.

If you perceive the situation you're in to be a traumatic event, you radiate trauma to yourself and all involved. If you think the situation you're in is an opportunity to learn a lesson and you take advantage of that opportunity, the event will be less traumatic than if you had thought otherwise. Take the example of a parent and child. The parent's reaction to the child tripping and falling affects the level of trauma from the perception of the child. If the parent's reaction is that it is no big deal, the child will often get up and go on with whatever they were doing. If the parent's reaction is panic, the child will likely cry and experience trauma from the event.

Your perception of a situation and the emotions triggered by that perception influence the vibration of the energy of that experience. This applies to your experiences and others' experiences. Your perception of *any* situation and the emotions triggered by your thoughts are the energy you radiate not only into that event, but into the Universe.

Where I feel this impacts the world the most—unfortunately, in a negative way—is in such situations as bombings at theaters, shootings at schools, murders, child abuse, etc. These events trigger very strong judgment and emotions of extreme anger, hatred, rage, fear, sorrow, pity, and grief, just to name a few. Remember that thoughts and emotions give energy direction and power. The thoughts and emotions that follow such severe tragedies are very strong and negatively impact the Universal energy powerfully. Perceptions of events such as these create *more* anger, hatred, rage, fear, sorrow, pity, grief, etc. in the Universe. Maybe that is why they seem to occur more often.

There is no way that the general population will ever be able to understand the perspective from which the assailant acted. Adding lower-level emotions to the event, especially the ones as powerful as anger, hatred, rage, and fear, does not help the people affected. In fact, because your perception and the emotions associated with that perception influence the situation and the people involved, it actually affects them in a negative way. They are experiencing a large amount of trauma on their own—they do not need anyone else adding negative energy to it.

Everyone involved, whether directly or hearing about it from the media, has spiritual lessons to learn. **Activate all lessons everyone is to learn from the experience. Transform all Sources of everything everyone is feeling to Unconditional Love & Unconditional Gratitude**™. Contribute to HEALING and radiate Unconditional Love & Unconditional Gratitude™ rather than anger, hate, rage, fear, etc. Help create more positive energy in the Universe rather than adding to the negative energy.

The best way you can positively help those affected both directly and indirectly is to apply the Infinite Healing™ tools.

**"I activate all lessons
that everyone is to learn from this experience."**

"I transform all Sources of sorrow, anger, and
everything else I am feeling about this situation to
Unconditional Love & Unconditional Gratitude™."
"I transform all Sources of everything everyone is feeling about
this situation to
Unconditional Love & Unconditional Gratitude™."
"I transform all Sources of that situation to
Unconditional Love & Unconditional Gratitude™."
"I transform all Sources of judgment to
Unconditional Love & Unconditional Gratitude™."

You can use this concept with *any* less-than-desirable situation. When I pass an accident, hear a siren, read or hear about a traumatic story, I immediately **activate all lessons that everyone is to learn from that experience** and **transform all Sources of that experience to Unconditional Love & Unconditional Gratitude™**. Remember, transforming all Sources to Unconditional Love & Unconditional Gratitude™ puts more Unconditional Love & Unconditional Gratitude™ into the Universe, so the more you can be reminded to transform, the more often you're transforming the energy in the world.

Just like your perception can affect the energy of the situation, others' perception can affect the energy of *your* situation. For example, in the case of an injury, if others witness your injury, their perceptions of the severity of your injury will affect the vibration of the energy of the injury, which can in turn affect the seriousness of your injury.

Here is an example of how others' perceptions of your experience can influence the vibration of your energy. I was carrying a box in from the garage through the laundry room and turned too quickly when entering the hallway. The box hit the doorjamb, and a corner of the box went into my left shoulder. I immediately repeated, "Nothing has happened." (You will learn more about the "nothing has happened" tool later.) Every time I noticed my shoulder hurting, I would say,

"Nothing has happened." I soon forgot what had happened and went on about my day.

That evening was bowling league night. During warm-up, I rolled several balls with no problem. As our team sat at the table waiting for league to begin, we were talking about silly things we've done and I told them about running into the doorjamb. There was laughter and comments like "Wow, that must've hurt," "Ouch," and cringes as I told my story. I decided to warm up one more time before league began. I picked up my ball, and as I was getting set on the approach, I attempted to lift my left arm to support the ball. Sharp pains went through my shoulder and I couldn't even lift my arm.

After some deliberation, I realized that I had "reactivated" the trauma of the event by telling my story, and their perceptions had influenced the energy of my event. I again repeated, "Nothing has happened," and shortly after, the pain went away. Note that this was in the early stages of Infinite Healing™. If this were to happen again, I would **activate all lessons that everyone is to learn from the experience** and **transform all Sources of the trauma to Unconditional Love & Unconditional Gratitude**™ as well as using the tool "nothing has happened." In hindsight, HEALING by activating all lessons and transforming all Sources actually could have prevented the energy from being reactivated.

This is why I recommend, "If no one witnessed the injury, don't tell anyone about it." Then it's only your perception you have to pay attention to.

Positive perceptions, whether they are yours or someone else's, energized with Unconditional Love & Unconditional Gratitude™, happiness, JOY, PEACE, etc. will make the outcome of any situation more positive. Negative perceptions, whether they are yours or someone else's, charged with fear, pity, blame, grief, shame, regret, resentment, etc. will make the outcome of any situation more traumatic.

The vibration of your energy influences everything around you. Negative energy makes plants die, electronics and appliances "freak out" or stop working, vehicles have problems, situations become more traumatic, and others feel negative. Negative energy is negative perceptions, negative thoughts, negative emotions, and negative intentions whether you're aware of them or not.

On the other hand, positive energy makes plants flourish, vehicles run seamlessly, appliances run smoothly, situations be less traumatic, and other people feel good. Positive energy is positive perceptions, positive thoughts, positive emotions and positive intentions.

What vibration of energy are YOU contributing to the Universe?

Your energy influences everything around you, and your energy affects everything you do. Whatever thoughts you're having and whatever emotions you're feeling at the time you do something is the energy that goes into what you're doing. For example, cooking in our house is never allowed if the cook is grumpy or mad. The energy the cook has at the time they are cooking is the energy that goes into the food. This also applies to art, gardening, driving, sports, working, paying bills, sewing, etc.

I think about this concept when it comes to "lemons." How can something made on an assembly line produce so many vehicles that run fine, but then have a few lemons? Is it the energy of an assembly line worker having a bad day, or the conversation of the workers while they are working on that particular vehicle? Maybe it is the energy of the transporter or the energy of the dealership. I regularly transform all Sources of the energy of vehicles, used items, appliances, etc. to Unconditional Love & Unconditional Gratitude™. Will it prevent all problems? Maybe, maybe not. Will it lessen the potential of having problems? It certainly can't hurt.

INFINITE HEALING™ PRINCIPLE #3: YOU EXIST AT INFINITE LEVELS

You exist at infinite levels, which is what I call your Infinite Existence™. It is all levels of your consciousness, subconsciousness, and unconsciousness. It is your past, your present, and your future. It is all that ever WAS, all that IS, and all that will ever BE. It is your spiritual (Spirit), your mental (Mind), your emotional (Heart), and your physical (Body). It is every cell, every molecule, every atom, and everything in between. It is every point of your existence, inside and out. It is the Universe. It is GOD within you. It is *all* of You.

Because you exist at infinite levels, all that ever WAS, all that IS, and all that will ever BE is *within* You! What is in the outside is on the inside, what is on the inside is on the outside, the macro cosmos is within the micro cosmos. You are within the Universe and the Universe is *within* You. The Universe holds *all* knowledge of anything and everything. Therefore, the knowledge is *within* You for You to know anything and everything you want to know. Because you have everything within You, You just need to learn to TRUST what's inside.

YOU EXIST AT INFINITE LEVELS—CONSCIOUSNESS, SUBCONSCIOUSNESS, AND UNCONSCIOUSNESS

Your consciousness, subconsciousness, and unconsciousness hold the vibration of the energy of all of your experiences.

Levels of consciousness equal degrees of awareness.

Your consciousness is everything you're aware of, such as your thoughts, your emotions, your beliefs, your judgments, your opinions, things you have learned, etc.

Your subconsciousness includes everything that you're not consciously aware of but that you can become aware of easily, such as your thoughts, your emotions, your beliefs, your judgments, your opinions, memories, phone numbers, names, colors, routines, generational conditioning, social conditioning, etc. The subconsciousness is primarily motivated by emotion, not reason.

Generational conditioning refers to beliefs, opinions, judgments, and traditions that have been learned and passed on from generation to generation. Social conditioning refers to beliefs, opinions, and judgments that have been learned from society, including influences from advertising, society's expectations, and society's viewpoint of what is acceptable and what is not. Generational conditioning and social conditioning are very closely associated and include such things as stereotyping, prejudice, and judgments. Generational conditioning and social conditioning create beliefs that you're often not even aware of, which can be stored in either your subconsciousness or your unconsciousness.

You interchange information from your subconsciousness to your consciousness regularly. If you need to remember a name or a number, you retrieve that information from your subconscious and consciously become aware of that name or number, and then it goes back to the subconscious for easy recall the next time you need it.

As you go through life, you create habits and routines. Take, for example, the pattern of getting ready for the day. You often do the same things, in the same order day after day. You have done things in that order for so long that you don't really think about what you're doing or what comes next, yet you "know" and you move instinctively through that routine. However, if the flow is interrupted, you may have to stop and think about what comes next or you may actually forget to do something.

You drive to and from work regularly. Have you ever experienced leaving somewhere and arriving at your destination, but you do not remember the drive? Your routines are stored in your subconsciousness.

Your unconsciousness is everything that you're not aware of that cannot be easily brought to your consciousness. The information that is stored in your unconsciousness is often why you behave or react the way you do. It also includes everything that cannot be remembered without a deliberate intent to go "there," or a trigger that brings something to awareness. That something may be a memory, or it may be an emotion. For instance, a loud screeching noise may trigger intense fear, and even though the person has no recollection as to why, the fear that they feel is real. The smell of a rose may bring about a sense of grief, relating to the emotion felt at a funeral. A song may remind you of a very happy time in your life, or of a very sad one. Your unconsciousness holds the energy of many experiences, such as traumatic events that have been suppressed, memories, past lives, thoughts, emotions, beliefs, generational conditioning, social conditioning, fetal development, etc.

If you experience something and have no reason to disbelieve or doubt the information, it can settle into your subconsciousness or unconsciousness as being TRUE, which creates a belief, which in many instances you may not even know is there.

The definition of "trauma" is relative to each individual. What may seem severely traumatic to one may not seem very traumatic to another. One person may suppress a traumatic event deep into the unconsciousness, but another may not understand why that particular situation would seem so awful. That is because the perspective of the person at the time of the event is based on that person's past experiences, beliefs, judgments, and his/her mental and emotional state at the time.

Sometimes, when past experiences move from your unconsciousness to your consciousness, it does not make sense why it would have been traumatic from the perspective from which you're viewing it now. For example, something that happened during childhood, which you then perceived as being severely traumatic, when you look at what happened now, from an adult perspective, does not seem that traumatic. Regardless, it was traumatic enough for you at the time to bury it deep into your unconscious. HONOR it and use the Infinite Healing™ tools to HEAL it!

During fetal development, the energy of the fetus is experiencing all the things that the mother is experiencing. Although the fetus does not have the capacity to formulate their own perspective of the situation, what they feel is the same thing as the mother feels. If the mother experiences anger, the fetus experiences anger. When the mother experiences JOY, the fetus experiences JOY. The experiences of the fetus during development are all stored in the unconsciousness. What a great reason to implement Infinite Healing™ during pregnancy.

To shift in the degree of awareness from the unconscious level to the conscious level, you must have an open Mind and consider perspectives and possibilities outside of your norm, outside of your comfort zone. You must be willing to go to unexplored places in your Mind. You must TRUST in the Universe, in GOD, and you must be willing to become aware of You.

The ultimate level of consciousness is a complete and unfiltered awareness of You—of what you think, of what you feel, of what you believe.

YOU EXIST AT INFINITE LEVELS—PAST, PRESENT, AND FUTURE

You are the sum of all your experiences—everything that has ever happened in your past, everything that is happening in your present, and everything that may happen in your future. Everything that has happened in your past influences your present, everything that happens in your present affects your future, and everything that has happened in your past influences your future. Everything that has ever happened in your existence is part of You, of your Infinite Existence™.

You are the sum of all of your experiences.

You Exist At Infinite Levels—Spirit

You *are* a Spirit—you do not *have* a Spirit. You *are* a spiritual being in a human Body. Each person's primary purpose of being here on earth is to grow spiritually. Each of you is on a specific course to enhance your Spirit by learning spiritual lessons, helping others, and making this world a better place. This is your Spiritual Course™, and it is made up of divine opportunities presented *for* You to help you achieve your primary purpose. It is the reason you encounter *everything* in your life—every event, every person, every interaction, every experience, every moment, every day, every minute, every second, whether you're directly involved or experiencing it from a distance, whether you experience it firsthand or hear about it on the television, radio, from another person, or read it in the newspaper or on the Internet.

How you accomplish your primary purpose varies from person to person, and is as individual as you are.

There are two things that will appear on your Spiritual Course™—blessings and opportunities to learn lessons and to HEAL. All positive experiences are blessings, and all less-than-desirable events are opportunities to learn lessons and to HEAL.

On your Spiritual Course™, the potential of *anything and everything* happening is possible—it is a Course where *all* possibilities exist. There are many different factors that influence what experiences appear in your life on your Spiritual Course™.

One of these is your consciousness. Remember, this is what you're aware of, including your thoughts, your emotions, your beliefs, your judgments, your expectations, your imagination, your dreams, etc. All of these *influence what appears on your Spiritual Course™*.

It is also inspired by your subconsciousness and your unconsciousness which consist of things that you're not consciously aware of but that are a very big part of you. This includes the thoughts, emotions, beliefs, judgments, expectations, etc. that you may not even know are there.

Your Spiritual Course™ is directed by what has happened in the past (all that ever WAS). This includes each and every experience in the past of this lifetime, and if you believe that each Spirit lives multiple lifetimes, by each and every experience in each previous lifetime. Your perspective of each past situation, the emotions that were triggered, and your actions or reactions at the time *influence what has appeared on your Spiritual Course™*. If you're still a victim of what happened in your past, it will continue to *influence what appears on your Spiritual Course™*.

> *Some of what appears on your Spiritual Course™ is what many refer to as* karma *or* fate. *Although most people associate this with negative behavior, it applies to both the negative and the positive. I have given this topic a lot of thought and have concluded that this may be why some people live more blessed lives than others, and this may be why some babies and children experience terrible things. Take, for example, Adolph Hitler. The things he did were undeniably horrendous and appalling. With his death, his Spirit was "freed" from his lifetime. Within the concept of multiple lives, his Spirit eventually came back as another person. All people begin their lifetimes as babies. So if his Spirit came back as a baby, what kind of energy does that baby come with? What kind of influence is the past going to have on the current lifetime? We generally view babies and children as being good and innocent. But the past does influence our Spiritual Course™, and we do attract what we give out. This does not mean that I believe that any baby or child "deserves" anything. I believe that each lifetime is an opportunity to enhance the Spirit, and that each and every baby born and each and every person provides another opportunity to HEAL the Spirit and make this world a better place.*

The most common use of the word "karma" is that
when someone does something bad, something bad will
happen to them. If someone "wrongs" you or someone
else, they will be "wronged"—maybe not now, maybe
not tomorrow, but someday. This comes from a victim
viewpoint that life happens to them (see Principle #7—
Life is NOT Personal). People actually hope that karma
is true and wish it upon others, generally from a negative
perspective. Would they wish the same if they knew that
negative karma may affect a baby or a child? A great
reason to teach young children the Infinite Healing™
tools and help them HEAL!

Your Spiritual Course™ is inspired by what is happening now (all
that Is). This includes your perspective of each and every experience
and the emotions triggered by those viewpoints, your actions and
reactions, your beliefs, your judgments, and your expectations.
Everything that is going on in your **now** *influences what appears on*
your Spiritual Course™.

What appears on your Spiritual Course™ is also determined by
what may happen in the future (all that will ever BE). This is also
where karma, fate, and destiny come in. There are certain things that
you need to experience that are orchestrated at a level far above your
consciousness. If you're meant to experience something specific, you
will experience it. If it is meant to happen, it *will* happen. Karma, fate,
and destiny *influence what appears on your Spiritual Course*™.

Your Spiritual Course™ is influenced by your Spirit, by how much you TRUST in GOD, in the Universe, that you're exactly where you're supposed to be at any given moment, experiencing exactly what you're supposed to be experiencing *for* You to accomplish your primary purpose. It is influenced by your Mind, which is your thoughts—your thoughts in the past, about the past, in the present, about the present, and about the future. It is inspired by your Heart, which is how you feel—how you have felt about experiences in the past, how you now feel about the past and about those experiences in the past, how you feel in each situation in the present, how you feel about your life now, and how you feel about what your future might be like. Your Spiritual Course™ is directed by your Body, which is your physical. How you feel physically has a significant impact on how you feel mentally and emotionally, and how you feel mentally and emotionally has a direct effect on how you feel physically. How you feel overall has a great impact on what will appear on your Spiritual Course™.

People are not given a good life or a bad life, as "good" and "bad" are subjective to each person's perspective. People are given opportunities to grow spiritually. Whether it is energy that has been carried from past experiences or whether it is the first opportunity to learn the lesson, *all* less-than-desirable experiences are opportunities to learn lessons and opportunities to Heal.

You Exist At Infinite Levels—Mind

From the opportunities presented *for* You on your Spiritual Course™, your consciousness creates perceptions of your experiences. Your Mind (with a capital M) is your thoughts about *everything*— situations, events, people, and even yourself. It is what you think.

Quantum physics says that it is the perception of the observer that creates their reality. For example, several people can witness the exact same scenario, yet have completely different views on what has happened. Remember that each person's perspective is based on his/her individual personal experiences, which means that it is *their* perspective that creates *their* reality. Each witness is right, in *their* reality, from *their* perception. Your perception is based on your personal experiences, which means that it is *your* perception that creates *your* reality. You are always right in *your* reality, from *your* perception.

Many of your perceptions are based on what you have learned they "should" be rather than what you actually think of the situation. These learned perceptions come from the way you are raised and include prejudice and judgment. Some come from society in the form of stereo-typing, advertising, media, or learning to think a particular way to fit in. Many come from your past experiences. When you experience a certain situation, your Mind creates a perspective of that situation. When you think about or experience a similar situation, you already have a learned perspective of what to expect. If your Mind does not know of another possibility, it tries to fit your experiences into what it *does* know. This makes your learned perceptions instinctive, which means that you think a certain way about a situation or a person often without intentional thought.

Do you think what you think because you've always thought that, or do you think what you think because it makes sense to You? Are you believing in someone else's truth, or is it Your truth? Becoming aware of what you really think is a critical part of HEALING.

You Exist At Infinite Levels—Heart

Your emotional body, your Heart (with a capital H), is your emotions. It is how you feel about situations, events, people, and yourself. It is one of the greatest things about being human and is a very powerful part of you. The moments that made a substantial emotional impact on you, whether it was positive or negative, are the moments you tend to remember the most. The people who made a major emotional impact on you, whether it was positive or negative, are the people you tend to remember the most, even though you may not remember exactly what they said or did.

What you think of a situation triggers an emotional response, which is how you feel about the situation and the people involved in the situation. Your feelings reflect and vibrate at the same level as your thoughts. When you have a negative thought, it triggers lower-level emotions (frustration, irritation, anger, sadness, disappointment, shame, regret, resentment, fear). When you have a positive thought, higher-level emotions follow (happiness, Joy, Peace, Love, gratitude).

Any time you feel a lower-level emotion, *it is for that time and all other times you have felt that emotion and suppressed, denied, or ignored it.* Emotions are often triggered by a current experience, but it is not necessarily the current experience that is traumatic. It is because those emotions have been suppressed, denied, or ignored before. That is why seemingly "little" things can set people off.

Remember that your thoughts are the **Sources** of your emotional reactions and determine what appears on your Spiritual Course™

and that your emotions always match the vibration of your thoughts. *You cannot have a negative thought and a positive emotion, just like you cannot have a positive thought and a negative emotion.* Even if you have a negative thought that triggers a lower-level emotion and you try to "counteract" the negative with a positive, the negative is still there— you're just denying or ignoring it.

Road rage, for example, comes from the perspective that someone has done something *to* you, or that someone has done something you perceive in a negative way, such as cut you off, pull out in front of you, or are going faster than you think they should. When you take their actions personally, the emotions that are triggered include anger, frustration, irritation, etc. When you have lower-level thoughts that trigger anger, you vibrate at the same frequency as anger (which is not high). Remember from Principle #2 that you radiate your vibration, and you attract the same level of energy as your vibration. When you're angry, you radiate and attract the same level of energy as anger.

Take into consideration, however, that most likely the way they were driving had absolutely nothing to do with you. They did not set out that day to find *you* and then wait for the perfect opportunity to pull out in front of *you.* I have a friend whose husband had a serious accident at home and his arm was bleeding profusely. She wrapped his arm in a sheet, loaded him into the car, and drove to the hospital. Did she dart in and out of traffic at high speeds? Absolutely! Did she cut people off? Probably. Was she focused on the other drivers on the road? Not at all. Was her intent to make them angry and ruin their day? Absolutely not! Her goal was to get him to the hospital as soon as possible. The way she was driving had absolutely nothing to do with the people who encountered her during that trip to the hospital. (Now, some of you might be wondering why she didn't call an ambulance rather than taking him herself. You think you know what you would have done, but you never know how you would react if you were in the same situation *unless you have had the exact same experiences and perspective of that person*).

Every less-than-desirable experience in your life, whether it is someone pulling out in front of you, someone making a comment that hurts, or a major incident, presents opportunities to learn spiritual lessons and opportunities to HEAL. Take advantage of those opportunities and apply the Infinite Healing™ tools to HEAL!

YOU EXIST AT INFINITE LEVELS—BODY

Your Body (with a capital B) refers to your physical Body, which is divinely designed to give you a mechanism to experience life. Within your Body, you have many physical systems such as your structural, digestive, and glandular systems, just to name a few. Although each system has a very specific set of responsibilities, *all* of them have been designed to work together seamlessly.

One duty of your glandular system is to translate your emotions into physical responses. This happens immediately and continuously. This is how your emotions change your physical DNA—positively or negatively. The emotions you feel either nourish or deprive your physical Body (positive emotions nourish, and negative emotions deprive) whether you HONOR them or not!

You have a physical Body—
you are NOT your physical Body.

When you do not know what to do with negative emotions, you instinctively suppress, deny, or ignore them, and they store in the physical Body. As long as they remain in the cells they continue to affect your DNA negatively, thus affecting all of your Body's physical functions. Lower-level emotions are *always* triggered based on your perception of what is going on. Lower-level emotions are the **causes** of disturbances in the Body, which create symptoms and eventually dis-ease.

Infinite Healing™ gives you a new alternative to suppressing, denying, and ignoring what you feel. Infinite Healing™ allows you to HONOR what you feel and gives you the tools to HEAL not only the emotions, but the thoughts as well. When you learn to use Infinite Healing™ to HEAL when you're in lower-level emotions, they do not have a chance to settle in the physical Body, and your Body has a higher possibility of staying HEALTHY.

INFINITE HEALING™ PRINCIPLE #4: YOU MUST HEAL AT INFINITE LEVELS TO TRULY HEAL

What if … it were possible to HEAL as if nothing had happened?

"HEAL" is not only one of the keys in Infinite Healing™, but is also the significant word in this principle. Remember that in Infinite Healing™ terms, HEALING means to restore to perfect health, to make WHOLE *as if nothing had happened.*

When you view yourself as parts rather than as a WHOLE you neglect very valuable sections of yourself. You ARE your consciousness, your subconsciousness, and your unconsciousness, so you must HEAL all. You ARE your past, your present, and your future, so you must HEAL all three. You ARE all that ever WAS, all that IS, and all that will ever BE, so you must HEAL all possibilities, all potentials that have ever been, that are, and that will ever be. You ARE every cell, every molecule, every atom, and everything in between, so you must HEAL all. You ARE your Spirit, your Mind, your Heart, and your Body, so you must HEAL all four.

HEALING YOUR CONSCIOUSNESS, YOUR SUBCONSCIOUSNESS, AND YOUR UNCONSCIOUSNESS

As we discussed before, when you're aware of something, you're conscious of it. You can be conscious of what you think, what you feel, what you believe, etc. The absolute best way to TRULY HEAL is to live life consciously and be aware of your thoughts, your feelings, your judgments, and your beliefs. If you're not aware that you have negative thoughts and feelings, you miss out on opportunities to HEAL. If you're not aware that you're judgmental, you overlook opportunities to HEAL. If you're not aware of your beliefs, you cannot be aware that you may have beliefs that do not serve you now. The best time to HEAL anything is when you're in it, but you must **be aware** that there is an opportunity to HEAL, and you must be willing to HONOR it in order to take advantage of it. Once you're conscious that there is an opportunity to learn lessons and to HEAL, **activate all lessons everyone is to learn from the experience** and **transform all Sources to Unconditional Love & Unconditional Gratitude**™.

> **"I activate all lessons**
> **that everyone is to learn from that experience."**
> **"I transform all Sources of that thought to**
> **Unconditional Love & Unconditional Gratitude**™.**"**
> **"I transform all Sources of** (insert feelings here)
> **disappointment and everything else I feel to**
> **Unconditional Love & Unconditional Gratitude**™.**"**
> **"I transform all Sources**
> **of judgment of myself and others to**
> **Unconditional Love & Unconditional Gratitude**™.**"**
> **"I transform all Sources of that belief to**
> **Unconditional Love & Unconditional Gratitude**™.**"**

Do you think what you think because an advertisement convinced you to believe that? Do you think what you think because you read something that told you that? Or do you think what you think because it is really what *you* think? Like you can be aware of your thoughts, your feelings, your judgments, and your beliefs, you can also be oblivious of these. When you are afraid of what you think, you instinctively ignore or deny your thoughts. When you do not want to feel what you feel, you unconsciously suppress your emotions. Sometimes they are repressed into the subconsciousness, but oftentimes they are buried deep into the unconsciousness. Are you one of those people who go through life completely blind to what *you* think, what *you* feel, and what *you* believe?

To intentionally HEAL the subconsciousness and unconsciousness, you must be intent on going to places you may have wanted to avoid before. This does not mean that you have to re-live a traumatic event. It does mean that you have to be honest with yourself about how you felt and how you feel about the experience. Sometimes this is a simple task, and as you think about the situation or replay it in your Mind, you can HONOR how you felt, **activate all lessons, transform all Sources to Unconditional Love & Unconditional Gratitude**™, and TRULY HEAL. Other times, as you think about the experience or replay it in your Mind, you may feel those emotions coming up again. It is important that if this happens, you *do not* suppress them again. HONOR them. Cry if you need to cry—scream if you need to scream. **Activate all lessons that everyone is to learn from the experience** and continually **transform all Sources of everything you're feeling to Unconditional Love & Unconditional Gratitude**™. Define the emotions if you can, but do not get caught up in trying to identify them. Take advantage of the opportunity to HEAL so you do not continue to carry the trauma with you any longer.

A great thing about Infinite Healing™ is that when you HEAL at the conscious level, you can also HEAL at the subconscious and unconscious tiers as well. That is why we transform *all* Sources. When you HEAL all Sources of anger, you're not HEALING only the Sources of the anger you're feeling now, but the Sources of anger from past experiences too. Is it HEALING all Sources of *all* anger that you've ever felt? I do believe this is possible. However, I have observed that many people believe that HEALING has to be a process and that it is not quick and easy. (FYI: HEALING *can* be quick and easy.) I have also noticed that many people have suppressed emotions so deeply that they do not HEAL all at once because they do not even know there are feelings buried.

> *You HEAL at the deepest levels*
> *when you HONOR You and*
> *when you HONOR*
> *what you really think and what you really feel.*

When you decide that you're finally going to listen to and HONOR your thoughts, you consciously become aware of what you think. Otherwise, you might try to keep your Mind occupied to keep those undesirable thoughts in your subconscious or unconsciousness such as focus on the positive, listen to the radio, watch television, read a book, or be occupied by your phone.

When you choose to pay attention to and HONOR your feelings, you intentionally become aware of *how* you feel, rather than instinctively suppressing those emotions.

When you decide that you're going be attentive to and HONOR what you believe, you bring to your consciousness what you *really* believe. Then you're able to assess whether or not *you* really believe that. Otherwise, your beliefs may sit in your subconscious or unconsciousness and interfere with you getting what you really want. For example, if you believe that people with a lot of money are selfish and rude, and you do not want to be that kind of person, your beliefs about those "types" of people may be getting in the way of you being financially abundant.

When you're aware of what you think, you're aware of your judgments. When you become aware of what you think, you see truth of who You are. When you allow yourself to HONOR how you feel, you can HEAL in the moment rather than suppressing the emotions and carrying that lower-level energy with you into the future.

Trying to address only parts of yourself, whether it is only focusing on your Body (physical symptoms), your Heart (emotions), your Mind (thoughts), or trying to improve your present is *not* TRUE HEALING and will only give you temporary improvements. If you want to TRULY HEAL, you must learn to view yourself as more than just your physical Body, more than just your emotions, more than just your thoughts, and more than just your life in the present. If you want to TRULY HEAL, you must learn to HONOR *everything* about who You are now.

HEALING YOUR PAST, YOUR PRESENT, AND YOUR FUTURE AND
HEALING ALL THAT EVER WAS, ALL THAT IS, AND ALL THAT
WILL EVER BE

HEALING your past is a critical part in TRULY HEALING your
Spirit, Mind, Heart, and Body as well as your life. Before Infinite
Healing™, you did not have the tools to HEAL, so you did what was
instinctive and you did the best you could with the knowledge you
had. Remember that releasing, clearing, or letting go of negative
thoughts and emotions may have helped you through some rough
times, but since it did not HEAL at the Source, there may be some
level of trauma remaining. To HEAL your past, **become aware** of
those times when you took life personally, when life happened *to* you,
when someone did something *to* you. Become aware of what you felt
and still feel about the situation. Even though you may now see how
that experience happened *for* You, it does not mean that the negative
thoughts and emotions you had at the time are gone.

To HEAL past traumatic events, you do not necessarily need to
know the exact emotions that were associated with the experience,
nor do you have to "load" the emotions you felt in order to HEAL
them. What you do need to do is be honest that it was traumatic, and
HONOR whatever you think and feel. If you begin to feel the emotions
again, do not suppress them. HEAL them now! If you do not feel the
emotions, do not force them.

After years of using the Infinite Healing™ tools continually
throughout each and every day to HEAL, I have found that what
triggers me most now are the actions and reactions of my family,
and I have come to the conclusion that this is a result of the many
years of missed opportunities to learn lessons and to HEAL because
I did not have the tools. This means, I have a lot of suppressed,
ignored, and denied negative thoughts and emotions, which have been
buried quite deep. I have also become aware that I tend to be much
more judgmental of family members than I am of others. Now that

I am aware of these facts, I have started HEALING and am making significant progress in this area.

One thing I do is to allow memories of situations to flow as I think of a particular person. Remember that intent matters, and it is my intent that everyone learn the spiritual lessons they are to learn and to HEAL any negative associated with the experience. If situations come to Mind and they were not positive, it means that it was an opportunity to learn lessons and to HEAL that I previously missed. The exciting part is that now I am taking advantage of those opportunities! So, I **activate all lessons that everyone is to learn from that experience** and I **transform all Sources of anger, disappointment, hurt and everything else that I feel or felt about that experience to Unconditional Love & Unconditional Gratitude**™.

Another way that I have HEALED the past is to think of a particular family member and HONOR everything I really think about that person. Yes, sometimes those thoughts are not nice but they are real, and if they are there, I might as well HONOR them and HEAL them so I no longer carry them with me. Let's say, hypothetically, that I view someone in my family as being selfish. **I activate all lessons that everyone is to learn from all experiences in which I have viewed that person as being selfish.** Then I **transform all Sources of everything I feel about that person being selfish to Unconditional Love & Unconditional Gratitude**™. I have done this for all family members I would have described as being selfish.

HONORING my TRUE thoughts and feelings about family members has nothing to do with my love for them. HEALING what I really think and feel allows me to love them unconditionally—for who they are and where they are at without taking their actions and reactions personally. I will continue to do Infinite Healing™ on my perspectives and strive to be able to see each and every member of my family from a place of Unconditional Love & Unconditional Gratitude™.

You can use these methods for more than just family members—you can use them for anyone you view from a negative perspective.

After you become aware and you Honor yourself, **activate all lessons that everyone is to learn from that person or experience.** Remember that learning lessons is one way we advance our Spirit, which is why we are here.

"**I activate all lessons**
that everyone is to learn from that experience."
"**I activate all lessons that everyone is to learn**
from that person (or insert name here)."

Now, **activate all Sources that allow you to Truly Heal.** If you feel that you're benefitting from staying angry at the person, you're in your way of Truly Healing. If you're holding on to anger, hurt, pain, disappointment, etc. as a "reminder" or a "protection" to prevent "it" from happening again (the "fool me once, shame on you; fool me twice, shame on me" concept), you're in your way of Truly Healing. Get out of your way!

"**I activate all Sources**
that create me to Truly Heal from this experience."

Next, **transform all Sources of everything you're feeling to Unconditional Love & Unconditional Gratitude™.** Do not filter your thoughts or emotions. If you thought it, Honor it. If you felt it, Honor it. If you still think or feel it, Honor it. It does not matter if it is nice—it does not matter if it is "socially acceptable" to think that way. Healing is between you and God, the Universe, and no one else. What matters is that you're Honest and True. If you do not Honor how you Truly felt or feel or that you were traumatized by the event, you *cannot* and *will not* Heal at the deep levels.

"**I transform all Sources of** (insert emotions here)
anger, frustration, disappointment, and everything

else I felt and still feel about that experience to Unconditional Love & Unconditional Gratitude™."

Grief over the loss of "better" times keeps you stuck in the past. It is impossible to create something greater if you're stuck in the past, even if you cannot imagine something better than what you had. If you "lose" something great, it means there is the possibility of something even greater. HEAL the grief and everything else that you feel and felt so you can become grateful for what WAS, and something even more wonderful can manifest in your life: **Activate all lessons everyone is to learn from the loss, transform all Sources of loss, grief, sadness, sorrow and everything else that you feel to Unconditional Love & Unconditional Gratitude™; then activate all Sources that create something greater.**

Do not obsess over what might have been. If it was supposed to have been different, it would have been. HEAL what you feel about what happened so you can stop carrying the trauma with you through your present and into your future.

Another great way to HEAL trauma from the past is to do small Infinite Healing™ sessions. Set aside 15-30 minutes. Go to a quiet, peaceful place where you can be alone with your thoughts. **Activate all Sources** that create HEALING in you. Then let your Mind go. Every memory that comes to Mind presents an opportunity to learn lessons and to HEAL. Even if you do not see how there could have been trauma, do not deny that there is an opportunity to HEAL. Sometimes when our older self looks back on childhood memories, we do not see how things might have been traumatic because we are now looking at it from an older perspective rather than the child's perspective we had then. It does not mean that it was not traumatic at the time.

For each memory, **activate all lessons that everyone is to learn from that experience** then **transform all Sources of trauma associated with that experience to Unconditional Love &**

Unconditional Gratitude™. Identify the feelings if you can, but do not get caught up in what you feel or felt.

If the memories flash through quickly like a slide show, allow them and HONOR them. Then **activate all lessons that everyone is to learn from all of those experiences** and **transform all Sources of trauma associated with any of those experiences to Unconditional Love & Unconditional Gratitude™.**

If you get stuck on one particular memory, it is likely that there is deeper trauma associated with it. **Activate all lessons that everyone is to learn from that experience.** Try to identify what you felt or still feel about that experience, and if you know there was anger, **transform all Sources of anger and everything else you felt or still feel about that experience to Unconditional Love & Unconditional Gratitude™.** If you know it was disappointment, **transform all Sources of disappointment and everything else you feel about that experience to Unconditional Love & Unconditional Gratitude™.**

If you cannot define it quickly, **do not** dwell on it.

> "I **activate all lessons**
> **everyone is to learn from the experience.**
> **I transform all Sources of everything**
> **I felt or still feel about the experience to**
> **Unconditional Love & Unconditional Gratitude™."**

As you become aware of and HONOR every thought that goes through your Mind, you'll find many of these opportunities to HEAL the past.

Each time you become aware of something in your past where lower-level thoughts and emotions happened, HONOR them and apply the Infinite Healing™ tools to HEAL so your past does not continue to affect your present negatively. If you do not HEAL it, it will stay in your energy until you do.

What if you woke up each day having learned the spiritual lessons you needed from the past, yet had no recollection of the *trauma* from the past? Infinite Healing™ creates that potential.

HEALING your NOW is crucial in TRULY HEALING your Spirit, your Mind, your Heart, and your Body, as well as your life. Now that you have the tools to TRULY HEAL all lower-level thoughts and emotions, there is no reason to carry the trauma of what happens in your present into the future. Live life consciously. Be aware of what you think *when you think it* and HONOR it. Be aware of what you feel *when you feel it* and HONOR it! HEAL the negative thoughts and emotions immediately, and you can create a wonderfully abundant future—in *everything!* Increasing your level of awareness and HONORING YOU creates TRUE HEALING at the deepest levels.

If it is a challenge for you to allow yourself to think what you think and feel what you feel, **activate all Sources that create you easily being able to HONOR YOU.**

"I activate all Sources
that create me to think what I think
and feel what I feel without judgment."
"I activate all Sources
that create me easily being able to
HONOR everything about ME!"

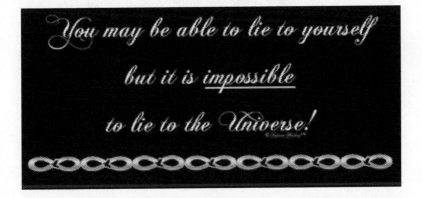

You may be able to lie to yourself
but it is impossible
to lie to the Universe!

Do not filter your thoughts or emotions. If you think it, HONOR it. If you feel it, HONOR it. Don't worry that it might not be nice—don't worry that it might not be what you "should" be thinking or feeling. What goes on in your head is between you, your Spirit, and GOD. You cannot lie to your Spirit and you cannot lie to the Universe. What makes the most difference is whether or not you're being HONEST and TRUE with yourself. If you do not HONOR how you TRULY think and feel, you *cannot* and *will not* TRULY HEAL.

If you do not listen to your thoughts because you're afraid or ashamed of them, you must HEAL the fear and/or shame in order to feel safe to think what you think.

**"I transform all Sources
of being afraid of my thoughts to
Unconditional Love & Unconditional Gratitude™."
"I transform all Sources
of being ashamed of my thoughts to
Unconditional Love & Unconditional Gratitude™."**
Activate all Sources that create what you want:
**"I activate all Sources
that create me to feel safe to think what I think."**

Each time you become aware of something in your NOW where lower-level thoughts and emotions happen, HONOR them and use the Infinite Healing™ tools to HEAL so your present does not negatively affect your future. If you do not HEAL it NOW, it will stay with you until you do.

As mentioned before, on your Spiritual Course™, the potential of anything and everything is a possibility. Each experience offers a new potential direction. Each experience influences what will appear next on your Spiritual Course™.

When you see a situation, you often have thoughts as to one or many potential outcomes. Take for example, the scenario of a little boy on a scooter who is turning a corner on the sidewalk and a big truck turning the corner on the road next to the sidewalk. What possibilities come to Mind? One possibility is each of them turning easily on their own route with no traumatic outcome whatsoever. Another is the truck turning too sharply, taking the truck up on the sidewalk and hitting or running over the boy. The potential of either outcome is real. The second one, of course, is not what we want to happen. When glimpses of such less-than-desirable outcomes run through your Mind, HEAL that potential by **transforming all Sources of that potential to Unconditional Love & Unconditional Gratitude**™. Then **completely TRUST that the outcome is exactly as it is supposed to be.**

> **"I transform all Sources of that potential to Unconditional Love & Unconditional Gratitude**™**."**

When you think about outcomes of your own personal situations, you often envision the results you want and even the one(s) you don't want. Then you fear that what you don't want is what you'll get. For example, have you ever been driving and you get a flash of an accident happening? When you foresee or fear possibilities you do not desire, HEAL those less-than-desirable potentials then **completely TRUST that the outcome will be exactly as it is supposed to be.**

> **"I transform all Sources of that potential to Unconditional Love & Unconditional Gratitude**™**."**
> Then **activate all Sources that create what you want.**
> **"I activate all Sources that create me to arrive safely."**

This does not necessarily mean that those lower-level potentials will not happen. It does mean that if they do occur, the result will be the best possible outcome for all involved. It also helps HEAL the fear associated with those less-than-desirable potentials and allows complete TRUST in GOD, in the Universe, that whatever happens is exactly what is meant to be. This is one way you HEAL your future. You also HEAL your future by HEALING your past, your present, and all of You!

HEALING YOUR SPIRIT

TRUE HEALING can only be achieved by HEALING your Spirit. When you HEAL your Mind, you HEAL your Spirit. When you HEAL your Heart, you HEAL your Spirit. When you HEAL your Body, you HEAL your Spirit. When you HEAL your Spirit, you HEAL your consciousness, your subconsciousness, and your unconsciousness. You HEAL your past, your present, and your future. You HEAL all that ever WAS, all that IS, all that will ever BE, and you HEAL every cell, every molecule, every atom, and everything in between. When you use Infinite Healing™, you HEAL your Spirit, and when you HEAL your Spirit, you HEAL your Infinite Existence™.

Your Spirit is the highest vibrating part of your existence and guides you in

*Spiritual HARMONY is the ability to flow in Unconditional Love & Unconditional Gratitude™ and enjoy life. It is having **absolute** FAITH and **complete** TRUST in GOD, in the Universe, in You. It is a **knowing** that life is **always** working **with** you, **for You**. It is the ability to navigate your life by your actions, but surrender the urge to control life. It is being able to experience life without having an attachment to the outcome. It is the ability to be loving in all situations, regardless of the circumstances (Unconditional LOVE); it is being able to be grateful for all opportunities regardless of the outcome (Unconditional Gratitude); it is a quiet embracing of what IS, without judgment. Most importantly, it is being aware that you have divine opportunities presented to you on your Spiritual Course™ and that you take advantage of those opportunities to HEAL along the way.*

life, on your Spiritual Course™. It *is* your direct connection to GOD, to the Universe.

Your Spirit always leads you in complete TRUST. Complete TRUST means that you are 100%, absolutely, without a doubt, certain that everything is exactly as it is supposed to be, that you *know* GOD is there with you through whatever you're going through, and that everything will work out just like it is meant to. No questions, no worries, no stress. It does not mean that you're numb to life or that you stick your head in the sand and just coast. It is total confidence in GOD, in the Universe, that life happens *for* You.

As mentioned before, you're on a Spiritual Course™ which is, in part, directed by your vibration (your thoughts and emotions). It is also guided by your actions and your reactions, which are directly related to what you think of each experience. There are only two things that you do in each situation—you either act or you react. Action is *taken* when life happens *for* You; reaction is *triggered* when life happens *to* you.

When you encounter less-than-desirable experiences and you view life as happening *to* you, you react with negative thoughts and emotions and you make decisions from a victim, lower-level viewpoint. When you encounter less-than-desirable experiences and you view life as happening *for* You, you take action and make decisions from a completely different position, from a higher vibration.

> ***Life is not intended to be difficult;***
> ***you really are meant to enjoy life and have fun!***

Your perceptions, beliefs, and expectations, your actions and reactions, your emotions, your vibration, and your destiny direct your Spiritual Course™. I have classified life into the following phases that you may experience at different times of life: BLISS, ENLIGHTENMENT, Awareness, The Rose Garden, the Scenic Route, Construction, and the Junkyard.

BLISS is the ultimate objective. This phase is where you always navigate your life (rather than try to control it); you always allow others to be who they are (without judgment); you accept who you are (without judgment); you always view life from a viewpoint of Unconditional Love & Unconditional Gratitude™ because life happens *for* You (rather than *to* you); you act (rather than react); and you infinitely vibrate at Unconditional Love & Unconditional Gratitude™. It is where you always feel awesome, Spirit, Mind, Heart, and Body; you live in Joy and in PEACE; you LOVE everyone and everything unconditionally; you're TRULY GRATEFUL for *everything* that appears on your Spiritual Course™; and you frequently smile just because. In this phase, you HONOR *everything* about yourself and others, and you have *absolute* FAITH and complete TRUST in GOD, in the Universe. You live in the Divine Light and Spiritual HARMONY.

The **ENLIGHTENMENT** phase is a *complete* level of consciousness where you HONOR all of You. You are aware of all opportunities to learn lessons and to HEAL when you experience less-than-desirable things in life—not just *your* life, but in all of life. This includes the less-than-desirable situations that you hear about or witness, and you take the opportunities to HEAL the energy associated with those situations. You *undoubtedly* understand the intricate connection between your Spirit, Mind, Heart, and Body. You are aware of every thought that goes through your head and you take the opportunities to HEAL all negative thoughts. You are aware of how you feel and you take advantage of the opportunities to HEAL all Sources of all lower-level emotions.

You are aware of your beliefs and you HEAL those beliefs that do not TRULY resonate with You. You are aware of your limitations, and you HEAL the things in your life that limit you. Life, for the most part, happens *for* You, yet you're aware of those times when life happens *to* you, and you take advantage of those moments to learn lessons and to HEAL. You act more than you react, yet you're aware of those times when you do react, and you use those times as opportunities to learn lessons and to HEAL. Judgment of yourself and others is minimal, you're aware of those times when you do judge, and you use them as chances to learn lessons and to HEAL. You navigate life more than you try to control it, you're aware of those times when you do try to control it, and you use those occasions to learn lessons and to HEAL. You live in HARMONY the majority of the time and you accept all opportunities to learn lessons and to HEAL when you experience dis-HARMONY.

You consistently feel great spiritually, mentally, emotionally and physically, and when you experience symptoms of any kind, you not only see them as opportunities to learn lessons and to HEAL, but you take advantage of them. In this phase, you HONOR *everything* about yourself and others, and you immediately HEAL all lower-level energy within your Spirit, Mind, Heart, and Body. You often smile because of the Unconditional LOVE you feel for someone or something, or because you feel an immense amount of TRUE GRATITUDE for something, anything, and/or because you're at PEACE. You are aware of the TRUE meaning of Unconditional Love & Unconditional Gratitude™. You know what it is like to often experience authentic JOY and PEACE. You live in complete TRUST more than fear, meaning you have immense FAITH in GOD, in the Universe, and TRUST that the outcome of every situation is just as it is supposed to BE. The fastest route to this phase is by TRULY HEALING your Spirit.

The **awareness** phase of life is one of the most exciting. You become aware of what you think and what you feel. You become conscious of not only how important it is to HONOR everything about YOU, but *how* to HONOR YOU. You begin to discover who YOU are now and how to HEAL the less-than-desirable things about yourself and your life. You are becoming mindful of the differences between life happening *to* you and life happening *for* YOU. You learn the difference between acting and reacting. You begin to see yourself as more than parts, and you start to understand the elaborate connection between your Spirit, Mind, Heart, and Body, your past, present, and your future, and your consciousness, subconsciousness, and unconsciousness. You learn the difference between navigating your life and trying to control life. You learn to live in complete TRUST and to be aware of those times when you live in fear. You become aware that life is an array of opportunities to learn spiritual lessons and to HEAL. As you begin to apply the Infinite Healing™ tools, you finally experience TRUE HEALING. In this phase, you discover YOU! The way to this phase is by living life consciously and by using the tools to TRULY HEAL!

In the **rose garden**, what appears on your Spiritual Course™ is mostly enjoyable, where every now and then you encounter some challenges (opportunities to learn lessons and to HEAL), but overall, life is pretty good. Life happens *for* YOU more than *to* you. You live in FAITH more than fear, and you act more than you react. You tend to attract good people and good things. You get here either by HEALING or by fate, which means that you may be aware of the opportunities to learn lessons and to HEAL and you take advantage of them, or you may be oblivious to how you're attracting what you have and you're just here.

There's the **scenic route**, where you tend to take your time learning lessons, advancing your Spirit in a round-about way where you experience some trials in life which I refer to as "construction" (opportunities to learn lessons and to HEAL). Life is just okay most of the time. You want to live in complete TRUST, but you're afraid to give up total control, so you bounce between FAITH and fear. You try to force the positive and deny the negative, which often creates a constant battle in your head. You force positive things in your life and avoid the negative. Sometimes life happens *for* YOU and other times it happens *to* you. Sometimes you take action and other times you react, and you try to control life more than you navigate. You will remain in this phase until you become aware that the challenges you encounter are trying to get your attention and get you refocused on your primary purpose.

In the **construction** phase, you may feel like you're facing challenges more often than not. You react more than you act and you're often negatively affected by others' actions because you take life personally. You try to force the positive or ignore the negative because you do not want to go "there." You suppress your feelings rather than HONORING them, but you do not often let them show, which means that what you show on the outside is different than what is really going on inside. Life happens *to* you more than it happens *for* You. You have low self-worth, you try to control life rather than navigate it, and you live in fear more often than complete TRUST, even though you're not necessarily aware that you're living in fear. The way out of this phase is to be conscious of your life, be aware that the challenges you encounter are actually opportunities to learn lessons and to HEAL, and use the tools to take advantage of them.

Then there's the **junkyard**, where few things ever seem to go right. Life is mostly miserable and feels like one big fight where you're continually experiencing struggle after struggle. In this phase, there is little-to-no JOY, little-to-no HOPE, and little-to-no LIGHT. You are a victim of life and you tend to blame others for what happens *to* you. Because you're a victim of everything, you do not want to go "there," which means you'll never HEAL "that." You feel as if life has given you the short end of the stick and is one giant disappointment. You react to life rather than taking action. You may be depressed or experience regular physical and/or emotional pain. You have numerous or serious physical ailments. You may have thoughts of suicide and sometimes think that the world or your family would be better off without you (note: the world would *never, ever* be better off without You!). You have low to no self-worth, although you do your best to show the world something different. You do not like to be alone with your thoughts and will do anything to avoid them (music, TV, games, alcohol, drugs, etc.). You ignore most feelings and just want them to go away. You may not be sure what happiness or JOY feels like, and you live in fear with very little-to-no FAITH. You may even doubt the existence of GOD. There may be flowers and other positive things in the junkyard, but they are often hard to see and are underappreciated, due to the desolate perspective of life.

If you're in or have experienced this phase, your Spirit is in critical need of HEALING! Sometimes the sunshine gets hidden by the clouds and rain, but that doesn't mean it is no longer there! The way out of the junkyard is to take action, increase your awareness, HONOR who you are, and use the Infinite HEALING™ tools to TRULY HEAL the things in your life that you do not like.

What phase are you in?

> *Remember, at any phase in your life,*
> *challenges and construction*
> *are opportunities to learn lessons and to HEAL!*

Your Spiritual Course™ may contain some or all of these phases at different times in your life, you may be in between stages, or you may be experiencing some of more than one phase. The times when you experience challenges or "construction" are gentle, divine opportunities for you to HEAL, *to get you back to the place where your purpose is priority, and where you strive to achieve your purpose.* When you get caught up in life's responsibilities and lose sight of why you're *really* here, you'll experience less-than-desirable situations. If you do not take those gentle, divine opportunities to learn the spiritual lessons you're here to learn and to regain your focus, you may eventually experience the junkyard. Remember that the junkyard consists of more drastic efforts to get your attention and **is a plea that your Spirit is in desperate need of HEALING!** There are no coincidences. *Every* lower-level thing that appears on your Spiritual Course™ is an opportunity *for* You to learn lessons and to HEAL!

There is *never* an opportunity to go the wrong way on your Spiritual Course™. It does not consist of forks in the road where your choices take you left or right. Your Spiritual Course™ is one long road that just appears, and what you experience *is* always the right journey *for* You at the time. Every negative experience provides an opportunity to learn lessons, to HEAL, and to advance your Spirit. Every person is one of GOD's masterpieces—YOU are one of GOD's masterpieces. GOD, the Universe, is *always* with you, encouraging you to vibrate higher, there for you without judgment, there for you to turn to when there seems like nothing else, there for you regardless of the choices you make, and there to divinely guide you when you're ready to listen. Remember that your Spiritual Course™ includes everything that you experience—every event, every person, every interaction, every thought, every emotion, every minute, every second, and regardless of what appears on our Spiritual Course™, the divine opportunities presented are *always—ALWAYS—for* You.

No matter what phase you're in or how long you've been travelling on your Spiritual Course™, it is never too late to HEAL and create a more JOYFUL destination.

The thoughts you have are directly related to your ability (or inability) **to flow in Spiritual HARMONY.** When you flow in Spiritual HARMONY, your Mind instinctively follows with positive thoughts. Your Mind is actually the map to your Spiritual Course™. This means that your perspective of the things that happen in your life influence the experiences presented to you on your Spiritual Course™.

Spirit	Mind	Heart	Body
Spiritual	Mental	Emotional	Physical
Course	Source	Cause	Symptom
Opportunity	HEAL	*Remedy*	*Treat*

Although it is the intention that your Spirit leads you in complete TRUST, it has somehow evolved that the vibration of your Mind has *the* most significant impact on your life.

HEALING YOUR MIND

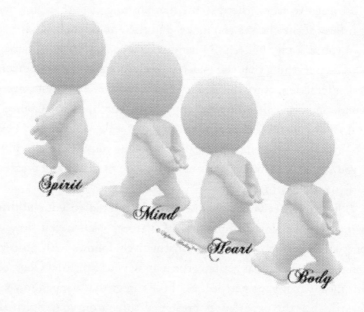

Your Mind instinctively follows your Spirit in complete TRUST unless you override your instincts and allow your Mind to lead in fear. You cannot live in complete TRUST and in fear at the same time. You are in either one or the other. Living in fear means that you're not sure that everything is exactly as it is supposed to be, and you're uncertain that it will work out the way you want it to or the way you think it should. Stress is based on fear. Worry is a degree of fear. Doubt is a level of fear, as is concern, uncertainty, anxiety, dread, distress, agony, dismay, distrust, and skepticism. Fear is having an attachment to the outcome. If you feel the need to protect you or your loved ones from something, you're living in fear. Fear is assuming that maybe you know what is better for you and others than GOD, than the Universe, does.

Where there is fear, there is *never* the complete TRUST that I am referring to. They do not, cannot, and will not co-exist. You live either in complete TRUST or in fear. Throughout your life, even throughout the day, you may shift from one to the other. The ultimate objective is to live in complete TRUST all the time, which allows your Spirit to lead. When you live in fear, you allow your Mind to lead.

When you have a thought, it is out in the Universe. The moment you have a thought, you have given energy direction. Wishing you didn't have the thought or telling yourself you should not think that way **does *not* negate** the thought or the energy of the thought. Your thoughts are there and are between you and GOD. Even though you may try to ignore or deny them, you cannot always completely hide your thoughts from yourself, and you certainly cannot ever hide them from your Spirit, from GOD or from the Universe.

> *Mental* HARMONY *is the ability to perceive every situation, every person, and every interaction from a viewpoint of Unconditional Love & Unconditional Gratitude*™. *If you perceive anything lower than Unconditional Love & Unconditional Gratitude*™, *it is an indication that you have been presented with an opportunity to learn lessons and to* HEAL. *When you perceive that life happens to you, it is an indication that you have an opportunity to* HEAL. *The only way to get to a state of Mental* HARMONY *is to take advantage of all opportunities to learn lessons and to* HEAL.

You must be willing to HONOR *your thoughts to* TRULY HEAL. Sometimes this can be a scary thing. I know. I have been there. I have been shocked and even ashamed at some of my thoughts. But you're human, and it is absolutely necessary for you to not only acknowledge that, but to accept it. Not all of your thoughts are pure, and that is okay. Sometimes you have negative thoughts and that is fine. Denying that you have them holds you back and keeps you stuck in the negativity. Ignoring them gets in your way of TRULY HEALING. Do not beat yourself up over what you think. Your thoughts do not have to define you. **It is *always* okay to think what you think.** Accepting this is the only way you can TRULY HEAL the negative.

Many have tried to program themselves to think positive, not to allow negative thoughts or to let go of negative people. Many have been taught that when they have a negative thought, they should counter it with a positive one, to focus their attention on what they *do* want rather than what they don't want. Positive thinking is a powerful tool, but when you force positive thinking, you often have a battle in your head between what you really think and what you want to think. In the process of forcing positive thoughts, you often deny or ignore the negative, and therefore miss the opportunities to learn lessons and to TRULY HEAL. When you stay away from or avoid negative people, you deny yourself opportunities to learn lessons and to HEAL. Whatever and whomever you have encountered has appeared on your Spiritual Course™ for a reason. Because every less-than-desirable thing that appears on your Spiritual Course™ is an opportunity to learn lessons and to HEAL whether it is a negative thought, a negative emotion, a negative person, or a negative situation, when you do not take advantage of that opportunity to learn lessons and HEAL, it will appear again, sometime, somewhere.

Positive thinking does not get rid of the negative. Positive thinking does not HEAL the negative. Positive thinking attempts to counteract the negative, which can make it an ongoing challenge. HONOR yourself by HONORING *all* of your thoughts. Then learn the lessons and HEAL the negative ones so positive thoughts can flow naturally.

> *You cannot live*
> *a TRULY positive life*
> *with a negative Mind*
> *(or pretending that you*
> *don't have a negative Mind).*

Sometimes in becoming aware of your thoughts, judgments, beliefs, etc., you may think that they show a kind of person you do not want to admit to or you do not want to be. Your thoughts, judgments, and beliefs have no more to do with the spiritual definition of You than others' opinions of You. Besides, ignoring or denying such thoughts, judgments, and beliefs does not mean they are not there. You may say that others' opinion of you does not matter, but in all honesty, it often hurts. HONOR it, **activate all lessons,** and **transform all Sources of everything you feel to Unconditional Love & Unconditional Gratitude**™. Learn to define yourself from a spiritual standpoint versus an ego-based one.

It is the Mind
that needs the most HEALING.

The sooner you become aware of your thoughts, the sooner you can TRULY HEAL the negative ones and the more often you *will* flow in mental HARMONY.

Spirit	Mind	Heart	Body
Spiritual	Mental	Emotional	Physical
Course	**Source**	Cause	Symptom
Opportunity	HEAL	Remedy	Treat

The Mind is the bridge between the spiritual and the emotional. The thoughts you have either nourish or deprive your Spirit and your Heart. When you have the perspective that life happens *to* you, your Mind instinctively follows with lower-level thoughts that trigger negative emotions like anger, frustration, irritation, sadness, disappointment, sorrow, fear, etc. which deprive you spiritually and emotionally. When you have positive thoughts, your Heart instinctively follows with higher-level emotions like happiness, JOY, PEACE, LOVE, and GRATITUDE, which nourish all of You, especially the Spirit. When you HEAL the Sources of the negativity in your life, positive things flow effortlessly. Becoming aware of when these opportunities arise and HONORING yourself in those opportunities is a critical part of TRULY HEALING.

> *The emotions you feel*
> *are directly related*
> *to the thoughts you think.*

HEALING YOUR HEART

Remember, Heart with a capital "H" is your emotional Heart, not your physical one. Your Heart *is* your emotions. It is how you *feel*. Remember that the emotions that you feel are based on your perception of the situation, positive or negative. When your perception is positive, the emotions associated with it are also positive. When your perspective is negative, the emotions that are triggered are negative as well.

As I said before, any time you feel an emotion, it is for that time and all the times you have ever felt that emotion and didn't know what to do with it, so you suppressed, denied, or ignored it. Emotions can be triggered by a current experience, but it may not be the current experience that is traumatic. It is because those emotions have been suppressed, denied, or ignored before, often many, many times. That is why something that seems trivial can set people off. This is what happens with people who take guns to theaters, schools, etc. It could be just "one more thing" that pushes them over the edge and makes them react the way they do. Yet another good motive to start HEALING!

Because we have never really known what to do with negative emotions, it has been passed down from generation to generation to suppress, deny, or ignore them. Teaching children of all ages to HONOR what they think and HONOR what they feel and giving them the tools to TRULY HEAL at young ages is a great way to make this world a better place! Imagine the possibilities of a world with less judgment, less anger, less fear, less resentment, less hurt, less disappointment, less frustration, and less irritation and a world with more Unconditional LOVE, more Unconditional GRATITUDE, more FAITH, more JOY, more PEACE, more happiness, more acceptance, and more laughter.

Like your thoughts, when you feel an emotion, the energy of that emotion is out in the Universe. When an emotion is triggered, it immediately gives energy power. Wishing you didn't feel that way, ignoring that you felt that way, or pretending that you do not feel that way **does *not* negate** the emotion or the energy of the emotion. It just suppresses, denies, or ignores it. Trying to let go of or release the emotion **does *not* negate** it. It just attempts to put it out in the Universe where it can then negatively affect someone or something else. If you cannot let it go or move on, you suppress, deny, or ignore it. Trying to convince yourself that you feel a positive emotion in a situation when you really don't **does *not* negate** the negative emotion. It just suppresses, denies, or ignores the emotion(s) you're really feeling. Even if you *are* able to release, clear, or let go of the emotion, the perception that you had that triggered the emotion is still there, which means that you're never able to transfer *all* of what you're feeling.

Contrary to what some may believe, you do not choose your emotions. You do not choose to feel sad, unhappy, etc. You feel what you feel because your thoughts triggered those emotions!

> *Do you choose to be happy, or*
> *do you choose to ignore the fact*
> *that you're unhappy and*
> *pretend that you're happy?*

You do not allow others to make you feel bad about yourself, angry, disappointed, etc. You feel what you feel because your perception of the experience triggered those emotions. That is why it is so important to learn lessons and to HEAL at the Source! You may not choose your emotions, but you do get to choose what you do with them. You can choose to suppress, deny or ignore them, or you can choose to HEAL them!

You must be willing to HONOR *your feelings to* TRULY HEAL. **The most opportune time to HEAL an emotion is when you're in it.** Are you hurt by a comment or action of another? It's okay to feel hurt. It's okay to feel angry, sad, disappointed, ashamed, guilty, irritated, annoyed, etc.

> *Emotional* HARMONY *is the ability to feel Unconditional Love & Unconditional Gratitude™ in every situation. If you feel anything lower than Unconditional Love & Unconditional Gratitude™, it is an indication that you have been presented with an opportunity to learn lessons and to* HEAL.

Do not apologize for how you feel. Do not try to justify why you feel the way you do. Do not deny or ignore what you feel. Do not wait until later. Do not force positive thoughts. Do not let it go, get over it, move on, be the bigger person, or release it. Take advantage of the opportunity to HEAL it *then*! Let yourself feel whatever it is you feel, *without judgment*. Then HEAL it by **activating all lessons that everyone is to learn from the experience** and **transforming all Sources of everything you're feeling to Unconditional Love & Unconditional Gratitude**™.

As mentioned before, when you feel an emotion it is for that time and all other times that you felt that emotion and suppressed, denied or ignored it. Like you feel it for all times, you *can* HEAL it for all times. If you're HEALING past trauma and you feel the emotion, HEAL it *then*! Do not wait until later. Do not force positive thoughts. Do not let it go, get over it, or release it. Take advantage of the opportunity to HEAL it *then*! In day-to-day life, be aware of what you're feeling and HONOR those feelings, *without judgment*. Take advantage of the opportunities to HEAL it *then*! Negative emotions feel much different when you feel it for that time only rather than for all times you've ever felt it and suppressed, denied, or ignored it.

Although the most opportune time to HEAL is when you're in it, you do not *have* to be in an emotion to HEAL it. If you've survived a traumatic experience once, why in the world would you want experience it again? I do not believe this is necessary in order to TRULY HEAL.

The experience provided an opportunity for you (and likely many others) to learn lessons and grow spiritually. You now have the tools to do that.

I discussed earlier that you can TRULY HEAL past trauma without loading the emotion or experiencing the trauma again. That being said, the most important part in HEALing past trauma is that you learn lessons and be honest with yourself that you were a victim and there were lower-level emotions felt. It does not matter if it makes sense or if it is logical. HEAL it by **activating all lessons** and **transforming all Sources to Unconditional Love & Unconditional Gratitude**™. If you can define what you felt or feel, do so. If not, do not get stuck in trying to.

> **"I transform all Sources**
> **of being a victim, anger, hatred, and**
> **everything else that I feel and felt**
> **about that experience to**
> **Unconditional Love & Unconditional Gratitude**™**."**

If, in the process of HONORING YOU, you begin to *feel* emotions, make sure that you allow them to flow and **activate all lessons you're to learn from that experience** and **transform all Sources of everything you're feeling or felt to Unconditional Love & Unconditional Gratitude**™**."** However, know that oftentimes it is possible to HEAL past trauma simply with the acknowledgement that it made you feel a certain way. You will only HEAL to the level that you're willing to be honest with yourself about what you feel and felt.

TRUE HEALING
does not mean the experience did not happen.
TRUE HEALING means that you HONOR everything
you think and feel about the experience and
are able to TRULY HEAL the trauma
so it does not continue
to negatively impact your future.

Thoughts give energy direction, but emotions give it strength. The stronger the emotion associated with the thought, the stronger the energy. Because you radiate and attract the same vibration as your thoughts and emotions at any given moment, it is important to allow yourself to HEAL past trauma so it does not continually impact your overall energy in a negative way. This is yet another reason that it is so important to TRULY HEAL so that you stop attracting things you do not want.

Spirit	Mind	Heart	Body
Spiritual	Mental	Emotional	Physical
Course	Source	**Cause**	Symptom
Opportunity	HEAL	Remedy	Treat

HEALING = *Activating all lessons and*
Transforming all Sources to
Unconditional Love &
Unconditional Gratitude™

Spirit, Mind, Heart, and Body are interconnected. What you *think* impacts how you *feel* both emotionally and physically. How you *feel* emotionally impacts not only how you *feel* physically, but also what you *think*. How you *feel* physically impacts both how you *feel* emotionally and what you *think*.

HEALING YOUR BODY

Physical HEALTH offers a freedom very few realize until one of two things happens—they either no longer have it, or they finally experience it. Sadly, there are many people who have no idea what being HEALTHY actually feels like. They do not know what it is like to feel good all day, every day, without taking medication for allergies, pain,

> *Physical HARMONY is the Body's expression of Unconditional Love & Unconditional Gratitude™, spiritually, mentally and emotionally. If the Body reflects anything other than perfection, it is an indication that you have been presented with an opportunity to learn lessons and to HEAL. In other words, every ache, every pain, every symptom is an opportunity to HEAL spiritually.*

high blood pressure, headache, or hormonal imbalance. It really is possible to feel good all day, every day, just because!

Remember that it is your Mind that triggers the emotions you feel, and it is your glandular system that translates your emotions into physical responses. Every emotion you feel has an *immediate* impact on the DNA of your physical Body, positive or negative, whether or not you HONOR those emotions and whether or not you recognize those immediate physical responses. In other words, lower-level thoughts trigger negative emotions which are the **causes** of *all* of the physical symptoms you experience. Consequently, your physical Body is merely a communication mechanism to tell you when something in your life is out of HARMONY and that you have lessons to learn and opportunities to HEAL.

> **Your physical Body**
> **is merely a representation**
> **of the TRUE condition of**
> **your Spirit, your Mind, and your Heart.**

What is your Body telling you?

When your Mind flows in mental HARMONY, your Spirit is allowed to lead in HARMONY, your Heart follows with positive emotions and flows in HARMONY, and your physical Body has no choice but to follow in HARMONY. This is the TRUE Spirit, Mind, Heart, Body connection.

> *The condition of your physical Body*
> *is directly related to the thoughts you think,*
> *the emotions that are triggered*
> *by those thoughts, and*
> *ultimately what you choose*
> *to do with those emotions.*

You can choose to suppress, deny, or ignore what you feel, or you can choose to HONOR what your Body is trying to tell you, learn your lessons, and HEAL all Sources of those emotions.

Spiritual, mental, and emotional toxicity create toxicity and disease in the physical. Any "inconvenience" or symptom in the Body is simply a warning to you that something is out of HARMONY in your Heart, in your Mind, and in your Spirit. If symptoms are masked or ignored, your Spirit continues to try to tell you that something is out of HARMONY and more drastic physical disturbances will appear. Masking or ignoring symptoms creates your Body to get further and further out of HARMONY, eventually creating more serious dis-ease.

Have you ever known someone who seems to eat all the right things, exercises regularly, and from a physical standpoint, appears to be very healthy, but they still get dis-eases like heart conditions, cancer, etc. or have heart attacks, appendicitis, or gallbladder issues? These situations are perfect examples of how if you only treat the physical, you *cannot* be TRULY HEALTHY, and that if you do not HONOR all of YOU, dis-ease will eventually follow. So, even though your physical Body is what you tend to pay the most attention to, it is simply how your Spirit tells you (bluntly or not-so-bluntly) that something is out of HARMONY. Will you HONOR it, or continue to ignore it?

How did we get so far away from Spirit

and become so anchored in the physical Body?

Maybe if we learned to see life as an opportunity to advance our Spirit by taking advantage of the opportunities to learn lessons, our physical Body would not need so much work.

You must be willing to HONOR *what your physical Body is telling you to* TRULY HEAL. If there are disturbances in your Body, there is dis-HARMONY in your Spirit, your Mind, and your Heart.

Dis-HARMONY *in the Body* =
dis*-HARMONY *in the Spirit, Mind, and Heart.

If there is sickness in your Body, it means that you have negative thoughts that triggered lower-level emotions that have stored in your physical. This applies if you experience only mild symptoms like a runny nose, headache, or nausea, if you have a cold or flu, or if you have a serious illness or dis-ease. Every physical symptom, no matter how minor, provides an opportunity for you to learn lessons and transform all Sources of spiritual, mental, and emotional disturbances that have been previously suppressed, denied, or ignored to Unconditional Love & Unconditional Gratitude™.

Although this topic is much more detailed than what we will cover here, specific negative emotions adversely affect particular organs. For example, bitterness stores in the gall bladder, all levels of anger stay in the liver, and fear disturbs the adrenals. If you have disturbances in the gall bladder, you *are* currently experiencing or suppressing, ignoring, or denying bitterness, *whether you can make sense of it or not.* So **activate all lessons** and **transform all Sources of bitterness to Unconditional Love & Unconditional Gratitude**™. If you have issues in the stomach, you *are* currently experiencing or suppressing, ignoring, or denying dread or anxiety, whether you can understand it or not. So **activate all lessons** and **transform all Sources of dread and/or anxiety to Unconditional Love & Unconditional Gratitude**™.

Your physical Body does not lie!

The more chronic or serious the condition, the longer you have been suppressing, denying, or ignoring You. Do not get stuck in trying to figure out or justifying why you felt the way you did or feel the way you do. Many times, the emotions that you feel will not make logical sense. If you felt it or feel it, HONOR it and HEAL it!

Your Body is an amazing creation that functions perfectly without conscious thought. It is so amazing, in fact, that you're not meant to notice your individual Body parts. How often do you remember that you have a pinky toe? A thumb? A gall bladder? An appendix? A stomach? A hamstring? Back muscles? You generally only notice your Body parts when they are hurting. If they are getting your attention in a negative way, there are lessons to learn and opportunities to HEAL.

The ultimate goal
is never to negatively notice
your physical Body parts.
That's when you know
you're flowing in HARMONY!

This does not mean that you *ignore* them when they are communicating with you. This means to HEAL when opportunities arise so your Body does not have to continually tell you that something is wrong and get louder and louder. If you happen to notice them without your attention being drawn to them, be grateful for them because every part of your Body is important to your life flowing in HARMONY.

Spirit	Mind	Heart	Body
Spiritual	Mental	Emotional	Physical
Course	Source	Cause	**Symptom**
Opportunity	HEAL	Remedy	Treat

Treating symptoms is significantly different than HEALING. When you treat the symptom, you may experience temporary physical improvements. When you remedy the cause, you may experience temporary emotional and physical improvement, but HEALING as a WHOLE is the **only** way to achieve TRUE HEALING. When you learn spiritual lessons and you HEAL all Sources, you'll experience long-lasting results in Spirit, Mind, Heart, *and* Body as well as in life. In fact, the only way to experience long-lasting physical results is to HONOR all of YOU!

The words "you" and "I" make things personal. Consider the phrase "People are HEALTHY." If we insert "You" or "I" in place of the general word "people," it takes on a new meaning. "You are HEALTHY." "I am HEALTHY." Now it is personal. Now it is about YOU. Do not make physical conditions or diagnoses personal. If you say "I have diabetes," you have made the dis-ease personal. A couple of things happen here. First, you have associated YOU with the dis-ease, and your Body is more likely to attach itself to the diagnosis whether it is a self-diagnosis or a professional diagnosis, and whether it is accurate or not. This is the same with "my allergies," "your heart condition," "his COPD." When you make things personal to YOU, your energy will follow with thoughts, emotions, and symptoms that fulfill the expectations of what you have personalized. If you feel you must associate with your physical disturbances, use a general reference such as "*the* allergies," "*the* diabetes," "*the* cancer," etc.

Secondly, when you make a diagnosis personal, you give your Body expectations of what it is "supposed" to do. Because the Universe knows all and your Spirit has direct access to this all-knowing field of energy, when you put a label on a disturbance, you create a belief system of what your Body is expected to do. If you label your disturbances as "my asthma," there are certain symptoms and expectations that are associated with the diagnosis. The Body now "knows" what it is supposed to do to follow the diagnosis. As long as you believe you have a dis-ease, the Body will do its best to live up to the expectations of your belief.

It does not matter what "it" is called. What matters is that your Body is communicating with you that there are lessons to be learned and opportunities to Heal and that you take advantage of those opportunities.

If a negative emotion is associated with the perception of an injury, the Body will respond with more physical trauma than if there is a positive reaction. This means that if you have anger or frustration related to getting hurt, your physical Body will react with more pain, more inflammation, and/or more bruising for a longer period of time. Any injury is an opportunity to learn lessons and to Heal, so make sure that you take advantage of them. **Activate all lessons that you're to learn from the experience** and **transform all Sources of anger, frustration and everything else you feel to Unconditional Love & Unconditional Gratitude™**. Also, **transform all Sources of the situation to Unconditional Love & Unconditional Gratitude™**.

You cannot TRULY HEAL at the physical level
if you do not HONOR
that you think what you think and
you feel what you feel.

94

Infinite Healing™ *does not try*
to make you a more positive person—
it HEALS the Source of the negative and
makes you an ENLIGHTENED person.

When you completely comprehend the Spirit, Mind, Heart, Body connection, you stop blaming others for the things in your life that you do not like or that you wish were different, and you stop blaming disturbances in your physical Body on what you eat and drink, activities that you do, or what you "have."

Listen to what your Body is trying to tell you.
It gives you clues as to what
needs HEALING in your life.

Hopefully, now you can see that *every* situation, every lower-level thought, every negative emotion, every physical symptom, every less-than-desirable person you encounter, and every less-than-desirable experience presents an opportunity to learn lessons and to HEAL your Spirit. Will you answer when your Spirit calls?

INFINITE HEALING™ PRINCIPLE #5: ENERGY FOLLOWS THOUGHT

As previously mentioned, energy is neutral and without reasoning capacity. It is thoughts and feelings that influence the energy and give it direction and power (your thoughts and feelings as well as others' thoughts and feelings). This means that energy *will* entrain to the vibration of the thought and the feeling. The stronger the emotion that is associated with the thought, the stronger the energy. Whatever you think about that has a strong emotion attached to it (fear, hate, Unconditional LOVE, Unconditional GRATITUDE) is where the energy follows *strongly and quickly*.

Your thoughts give energy direction, which means that energy follows thought. This is where the power of affirmations comes into play because when you think about something you want, the energy follows. On the flipside, when you think of things you don't want, the energy also follows, whether you HONOR those thoughts or not.

As stated earlier, *all* possible outcomes exist on your Spiritual Course™, and the potential of *anything and everything* happening is possible. And because energy follows thought, when you think about a potential outcome, whether it is one you want or one you don't want, the energy follows and increases the possibility of that outcome happening. Changing your thoughts to a possible outcome you prefer does *not* negate the direction of the potential you didn't want. So if a potential outcome crosses your Mind that you do not want, make sure you **transform all Sources of that potential to Unconditional Love & Unconditional Gratitude™**. This HEALS that potential so that if it *does* occur, it will create the best possible outcome for all involved. If you want a situation to happen a certain way, **activate all Sources that create it**. Then get out of the way and TRUST that whatever outcome happens is the best one *for* everyone involved. If you do not use the Infinite Healing™ tools, either transforming or activating all Sources, then you leave the outcome up to chance, and the energetic vibration of those involved at that time will have a more significant effect on the result.

Since energy follows thought, if you're saying one thing, but your Mind thinks or doubts that what was said is true, the energy will follow what your Mind is thinking. The energy will *always* flow stronger with what you believe to be true rather than what you say. For example, if you state the affirmation that "I am financially abundant" but your Mind has doubts or disagrees, the affirmation is negated. If you simply focus on the positive and think "I am healthy" but you don't feel healthy, the power of the energy of the positive thought is weakened or negated, and the energy now goes to the *knowing* that you're not healthy.

You can (try to) *lie to yourself,*
but it is impossible *to lie to the Universe!*

Many have been taught to focus on the positive, to focus on the things they want. If you have a negative thought or have a thought about something you don't want, you may have trained yourself to change that thought and think about what you *do* want. This has worked well for some. For others, it becomes a constant battle to change your thoughts or to keep your focus on the positive.

Forcing positive thoughts and
positive emotions and
only focusing on the things you do want
is denying the negative and
ignoring the reason
you do not already have what you want.
This is NOT Honoring You!

Forcing positive thinking is masking the symptom, ignoring the Source, and dis-Honoring You. If you think it, it is real. If you feel it, it is real. If it matters to you, it matters. Telling yourself that it isn't or shouldn't be important does not mean that it really isn't important. Pretending it is not significant does not mean it isn't.

Learn to HONOR YOU by HONORING your thoughts and HEALING all Sources of the ones you do not want. HONOR yourself by HONORING the emotions you feel and HEALING all Sources of the ones you do not like. HONOR yourself by HEALING all Sources of the negative and HEALING all Sources of the reasons you do not already have what you want. This is the fastest way to get what you *do* want!

Because energy follows thought, toxic thoughts create and attract a toxic environment, inside and out. HARMONIC thoughts attract and create a HARMONIC environment, inside and out. The only way to HEAL toxicity is to learn the lessons you're to learn and transform all Sources of negativity to Unconditional Love & Unconditional Gratitude™.

And since energy follows thought, your beliefs leave little chance for something different. The Universe will find a way to make happen what you believe will happen and present those opportunities in your life, positive or negative.

> *"It's always something."*
> *"It's Murphy's Law (if something can go wrong, it will go wrong)."*
> *"I always get sick this time of year."*
> *"When it rains, it pours."*
> *"My allergies always begin in July."*
> *"Business is always slow during the holidays (or this time of year)."*
> *"I'll gain weight if I eat this."*
> *"I always attract that type of person."*
> *"This always happens to me."*
> *"This country is falling apart."*
> *"The government is out of control."*

**The Universe may just give you
exactly what you expect it to.**

Become aware of what you expect. **Activate all lessons that everyone is to learn from those expectations.** HEAL your life by **transforming all Sources** (of things you do not want) **to Unconditional Love & Unconditional Gratitude™.** Then navigate your life by **activating all Sources that create what you want.**

*To see the results
of your past thoughts and emotions,
look at your current life.
It is your past attitudes, beliefs,
thoughts, habits, and actions
—and the emotions associated with them—
that have created the life you're living now.*

*More importantly,
to see your future, look at your current life.
It is your current attitudes, beliefs,
thoughts, habits, and actions
—and the emotions associated with them—
that are creating your future.*

You do not have to "live with" what you have created so far. If your current life is not what you want it to be, not what it "should" be, or not what you thought it would be, it is time to evaluate your current attitudes, beliefs, thoughts, habits, and actions and the emotions associated with them. If your life is not what you want, the time is NOW to begin to create a HEALTHY future, which is anything beyond this moment.

Dare to create something different!

Understand that Infinite Healing™ is **not** about *not* having negative thoughts and always keeping your thoughts positive. Infinite Healing™ is about HONORING the negative and HEALING all Sources of any negative. You are human, and negative thoughts reveal nothing more than opportunities to learn lessons and to HEAL. As I said many times before, it is *always* okay to think what you think, feel what you feel, and be who you are. Be HONEST with yourself about who you are now so you can allow yourself to HEAL and reveal the most amazing You.

When you HEAL all Sources of negative emotions, you have fewer and fewer negative thoughts. When you HEAL all Sources of what creates what you don't want, you get more of what you *do* want. When you HEAL at infinite levels, positive thoughts flow effortlessly.

INFINITE HEALING™ PRINCIPLE #6: WHAT YOUR MIND BELIEVES CREATES YOUR REALITY

Your Mind is a powerful thing. It cannot tell the difference between what is "real" and what is imagined. If it occurs in your Mind, it is "real." This includes every thought, every belief, every judgment, every daydream, every movie, every video game, every visualization—everything and anything that you *think* of. *This* is how your Mind extends beyond this dimension. And because your thoughts give energy direction, *this* is how your Mind continually influences the world.

> *Infinite Healing*™
> *produces results that will sometimes*
> *amaze and boggle the Mind,*
> *and it does not always make sense.*
> *Because it does not always make sense,*
> *it can be difficult for people to understand.*
> *Infinite Healing*™ *does not often fit*
> *into the box of human logic,*
> *nor does it fit into society's conventional box.*
> *But when given a chance,*
> *Infinite Healing*™ *provides unlimited potential*
> *to what you can experience*
> *if you'll open yourself up*
> *to a different perspective*
> *and if you allow it.*

A belief is described as a state or habit *of mind* in which trust is placed. Beliefs can be conscious, subconscious, or unconscious. Your beliefs are developed from family, friends, society, and your experiences. Beliefs are nothing more than opinions that you trust and are often passed down from generation to generation. Beliefs are hereditary. Beliefs are very powerful and give energy very strong direction and force.

If you experience something or are told something and have no reason to dis-believe or doubt the information, it can settle into your subconsciousness or unconsciousness as being TRUE, which creates a belief that in many instances you may not even know is there.

Ask yourself: Is it *our* belief, or is it *my* belief? Does that belief resonate with *me*? Does that belief make sense to *me*? Is that belief worth *me* believing in?

Actions that are not rooted in Unconditional Love resonate at a low-level. These include behaviors such as stealing, lying, abusing children or animals, selling or buying people as property, and discriminating against others. The mentality that claims it is okay to do such things comes from low-level attitudes. Although one may be able to justify to themselves that these actions are okay, they are never ethical. This means that beliefs like these generate a conflict between your Mind and your Spirit, whether you're aware of that conflict or not.

Low-level beliefs never HONOR your Spirit.

What if we **activated all lessons that everyone was to learn from low-level beliefs** and **transformed all Sources of the mentality that creates abuse, human trafficking, discrimination, poverty, starvation, dis-ease, cancer, etc. to Unconditional Love & Unconditional Gratitude™**? Imagine the kind of world *that* would create!

If you discover a belief within you that does not resonate as being TRUE to you, just deciding to change your belief may not be so easy. You may have to HEAL the old belief before a "new" belief can become TRUE. **Activate all lessons that everyone is to learn from that old belief, transform all Sources of the old belief to Unconditional Love & Unconditional Gratitude™, and activate all Sources** that create the "new" belief to be TRUE within you.

Some beliefs are so deep-seated that you may unconsciously believe something you accepted as being TRUE in the past, even if you're not aware of that belief or you think you're neutral on the topic.

Let's say, for example, as a child you were in the garden picking cucumbers with your mother. Your mother says, "I don't like cucumbers because they make you burp." You may have established an unconscious belief at that time that cucumbers make you burp. Now, as an adult, you still avoid cucumbers because sure enough, every time you eat them, you burp. Is it the properties of the cucumber that make you burp or your belief that cucumbers make you burp? This is another reason to become aware of what *you* believe.

> **Sometimes the things**
> **that may or may not seem TRUE**
> **are the things we need to believe in the most.**

You develop your beliefs from your experiences. This includes your own personal experiences as well as experiences of those in your life. If a child witnesses racism, especially from someone they hold in high regard (like a mother, father, grandparent, etc.), they learn to believe that judging someone for the color of their skin or for the slant of their eyes or for their nationality is okay. If you learned that money is always a struggle, financial abundance may be difficult to come by. If you perceived or were told that you were never good enough, you might believe that you're not good enough. If one day you ate tomatoes and got heartburn, you may have developed a belief that tomatoes cause heartburn. Therefore, each time you eat tomatoes you experience heartburn.

On the other hand, if you have been able to find a job effortlessly, you believe that getting a job is easy. If you have always had the money you needed, you may never doubt that you'll always have the money you need. If you pick up on new things quickly, you believe that learning is easy.

What you cannot understand is difficult for you to consider possible. If you have never been let down by the medical profession, being open to natural alternatives may not be imaginable. If you have never been in a manipulative or abusive relationship, trying to understand why someone else would stay in such a relationship may not make sense. If you have never considered suicide, you'll never understand why someone would commit such an act. If you have not experienced something *from the same perspective,* it may never make sense to you. Have you ever had an experience that made you see a different side of a potential, and now others' reactions in the same situation make sense?

What you believe can change in an instant.

Some of our beliefs create limits in our life. In fact, limits in life are set only by the narrow and logical thinking of the human Mind. The limits in *your* life are only set by what goes on in *your* Mind.

Sometimes, if you're not able to make sense of something, you do not understand how it could be possible. If you do not know of another possibility, your Mind instinctively tries to fit your experiences into something you do know, which are limited to your past experiences, and sets expectations from those experiences. When you view life from the boundaries in your Mind, you limit yourself in what you allow yourself to experience. When others tell you that you cannot do something or that the outcome of something is going to be a certain way, and you believe it, *you* are the one who limits yourself.

Understand that there is a difference between fear and caution. Fear is described as "a distressing emotion aroused by impending danger, evil, pain, etc., whether the threat is real *or imagined*." Fear is often based on the chance that the outcome of a situation will be unfavorable. For instance, if you do not get a flu shot, you fear that you might get the flu. If you don't hear from a loved one when you expect to, fear sets in that something bad has happened. If a young child is climbing on a ladder, fear is triggered that the child might fall.

Fear keeps you stuck in the negative, and because fear is a very strong emotion, it gives strong power to the less-than-desirable potential.

Caution, on the other hand, is a message to be careful. It allows movement forward. If you have an uneasy feeling about something, **transform all Sources of the fear to Unconditional Love & Unconditional Gratitude**™. If you still feel uneasy, it could very well be caution. If you have an uneasy feeling about something and you do not transform all Sources, you may misinterpret fear as caution and react accordingly. Decisions based on fear are often made in desperation. Decisions based on caution are generally much more reasonable. Caution allows you to take action whereas fear triggers re-action.

Your comfort zone is, well—comfortable. It is safe because it is what you know. What prevents you from stepping outside of that comfort zone is often the fear of the unknown. What if the unknown is better than what you know?

Life is AWESOME
outside of your comfort zone!

Understand that you do not have to accept the limits others place on you. Also know that you do not have to keep the limits you may have previously set for yourself. You are the only one who can limit yourself, and you're the only one who can remove those limits.

When you live with limitations,
you live limited experiences.

Perception occurs in the Mind and is a key factor in whether life happens *to* you or *for* You, and whether your life flows in Harmony or if it is a struggle. Others may see a situation different than the way you see it, but that does not make it wrong or right. It is just different. Each individual person's perspective is based on his/her experiences, which creates his/her reality.

Additionally, each person's **belief** is *his/her* reality. Whatever you believe is true is TRUE for you. What others believe is true is TRUE for them.

When people give you advice, it is based on their experiences and their beliefs. They will tell you what they think is right based on *their* perception of *your* situation. It is difficult for people to see beyond their own experiences. What is best for someone else will not always be best for *you*. What is best for you will not always be what is best for your child, your parent, your spouse, your friend, or your client.

Just like it is difficult for people to see beyond their own experiences, it is also challenging for us to see beyond the choices we do not understand, but it does not mean that those choices are "wrong." Others are traveling their Spiritual Course™ just like you're traveling yours. The experiences they need to advance their Spirit will appear on their Spiritual Course™ *for them*. They are not necessarily the same experiences that *you* need to experience on your Course.

Be cautious of judging another's situation based on how you think you would react or what you think you would do. If you have never been addicted to nicotine, it is difficult to understand why people would smoke. If you have never been dependent on alcohol, it is hard to comprehend the actions of an alcoholic. You *think* you know how you would react or what you would do, but it is difficult to know how you would react in that same situation if you had the same experiences of that person and were viewing it from the other person's perspective. This applies to your children, your parents, your friends, your siblings, your spouses or significant others, your bosses, your employees, etc.

Your life will flow much easier when you can accept that people see things differently and understand that *their* choices and *their* actions (or reactions) are based on *their* Spiritual Course™ and not yours. Remember, though—if you encounter them, they are on *your* Spiritual Course™ for a reason, so if lower-level thoughts and emotions are triggered because of the encounter, **activate all lessons that everyone is to learn, transform all Sources to Unconditional**

Love & Unconditional Gratitude™, and allow them to experience their own Course. Life makes more sense when you remember that the things that appear on anyone's Spiritual Course™ are always *for* them to grow spiritually, and if you encounter them, it is *for* You to advance your Spirit.

> *At the instant you experience something,*
> *your Mind has interpreted it*
> *based on your past experiences,*
> *not necessarily from what Is or what could Be.*
> *It is possible to consider a new perspective*
> *by using the Infinite Healing™ tools.*

One of the many amazing things about your Body is muscle preset. When you're about to perform a task, your Body prepares itself for what is coming based on what you *think*. For example, you go to grab a non-see-through carton of juice. You think you know how much juice is in the carton based on the last time you used it. Your Mind presets your muscles to lift that weight. If you think it is full but it is lighter than expected, you almost throw it as you lift it up. If you think it is close to empty but it contains more than you thought, you're caught off guard by the "extra" weight. If you do not know how much is in there, there is no expectation, so there is no muscle preset. If you think you'll be sore because you have not used "those" muscles in a while, those muscles will most likely be sore. If you think you'll experience pain because of repetitive motion, your Mind will preset your Body to comply. What your Mind believes creates your reality.

What if you became aware of what you think and what you preset *your* Body to do? What if you changed the expectations of what your Body will do? Then you just might be surprised at what your Body *won't* do.

This preset action applies not only to the muscles in your Body, but to *everything* in your Body, including your organs all the way down to the deepest levels of your being (every cell, every molecule, every atom and everything in between). If you think you'll be dragging after only getting five hours of sleep, you most likely will feel exhausted. Remember that fear gives power to a potential, so if you are afraid that you may get sick from coming in contact with someone who is sick, then your Body will often comply.

Again, if you have never experienced another possibility, your Mind instinctively tries to fit your experiences into something you do know, which are past experiences, and sets expectations from them. Preset occurs based on what you expect from your past experiences. If you get sick after eating a certain food, you tend to stay away from that food because of the "connection" it had when you threw up, even if it had nothing to do with you getting sick. If you worked out and were sore because of it, the expectation of being sore the next time you work out is high, which means that you'll likely be sore.

There are many times when I have experienced the power of my Mind and this preset function. When we decided to paint the trim on our house, I was up and down the ladder. Toward the end of the day, I became aware that my legs were getting a little sore. I had subconsciously thought that they would be sore, since going up and down a ladder was not something I do regularly. Knowing about preset, I **transformed all Sources of expecting soreness to Unconditional Love & Unconditional Gratitude™**. The soreness stopped and I never had another symptom, not even the next day when I was up and down the ladder again. The same thing happened with my arm. Because I was primarily using my right arm, I realized that I was almost expecting my arm muscles to be sore because of raising my arm above my head and the repetitive motion of painting. Once I became aware of what my expectations were, I **transformed all Sources of the potential that my arm muscles would be sore to Unconditional Love & Unconditional Gratitude™**. I did not experience any soreness or pain in my arm at all because I HEALED my lower-level expectations.

What your Mind believes creates your reality. Therefore, what you believe about your Body is important. Is it aged? Is it worn out?

Does it hurt all of the time? Does it fall apart as you get older? Be cautious of what you believe and be aware of what you expect because you could leave little chance for your Body to be something different. Besides, your Body can *never* flow in HARMONY when you have lower-level thoughts about any part of it.

Become aware of what *your* Mind believes. Become aware of what *your* Mind expects. What have you created in *your* physical Body from what your Mind believes or expects?

> *If only you could realize*
> *the power of your Mind…*
> *Then you could realize*
> *the amazing power of You!*

To accomplish what your Body instinctively does without conscious thought is beyond amazing—it is astounding. This includes things like breathing, digesting, heart beating, blood circulating, excreting toxins, healing a cut—only to name a *few*. Your Body is indeed wonderfully made. Never, ever underestimate the power of *your* Body to HEAL!

The Mind imagines the future just like the past and makes decisions accordingly. Only your Spirit can see past your experiences and your memories. What if it were possible to learn easily? What if it were possible to have a wonderful, loving relationship? What if it were possible to HEAL, even though there was an accident or injury? What if there is another way? What if being HEALTHY was easy? What if you dared to experience the power of You?

Are you aware of what you perceive? How often do you think about what you think about? Whether the glass is half empty or half full is based on *your* perception—either way, you're *right!* When you're conscious of every thought that goes through your Mind and you HONOR each and every one of them, your path to ENLIGHTENMENT and BLISS is much easier and faster. When you're aware of every thought that goes through your Mind, you get to know YOU at a very intimate level. And, when you're mindful of every thought that goes through your Mind, you can take advantage of those divine opportunities to learn lessons and to HEAL the YOU, you are now and finally reveal the YOU that *is* TRUE. It is a very empowering experience to discover the TRUE YOU.

Your Mind is a powerful thing, and what *your* Mind believes creates *your* reality. What are *you* creating with *your* Mind?

INFINITE HEALING™ PRINCIPLE #7: LIFE IS *NOT* PERSONAL

Everything that happens in your life is personal to *you* because it is your life. Everything that happens in others' life is personal to *them* because it is their life, but life is not intended to be personal. In fact, things other people *do* are rarely about *you!* The more often you can understand and remember this, the more often *your* life will flow in HARMONY.

It seems that in our world today, people tend to think that everything is about them. They instinctively take other people's actions personally, which triggers negative emotions. When someone cuts you off in traffic or speeds by you, weaving in and out of traffic, you may feel like that person did that *to* you. When other people don't do things the way you want them done or the way you think they should be done, you may take offense to it, as if the other person was not as intelligent. Taking life personally creates disappointment, anger, frustration, irritation, etc. even though things that the other person did had *absolutely nothing to do with you.*

> *You never know what
> is going on in someone else's world.*

Many people are completely unaware that the things *they* do may not be the best for other people, but are so concerned with what happens in their own lives that they do not consider how their actions and reactions affect others. Taking life personally makes you the victim of other people's actions.

> *Are you one of the many
> who go through life reacting?*

For example, I'm driving along and someone pulls out in front of me. That person did not set out to target *me*, Stacie Farnham. Maybe it was a new driver who thought they had room, or maybe they were distracted by thoughts of personal problems. There are so many scenarios that we cannot always understand. But instinctively, the actions of the other driver trigger anger, frustration, etc. because we have learned to take life personally. **Activate all lessons everyone is to learn from the experience** and **transform all Sources of everything you're feeling to Unconditional Love & Unconditional Gratitude™**.

Other people's actions
rarely have anything to do with YOU!

As I have said, it can be challenging for us to see beyond our own perception because we assume that everyone is just like us in the ways we think and believe. We instinctively see other people's situations through our perceptions and we react as if everyone thinks like we do. If we have a great work ethic we find it hard to understand those who do not. If we are honest we find it offensive to encounter those who are not. If we would never do "that," we find it appalling that someone else would. We rarely understand, or even consider, what perspectives others are acting from because what *we* know is the only way we know.

Common sense is based on
each person's perspective and
his/her experiences.
That is why common sense
may not seem so common.

Have you ever heard of the saying, "Trying to understand others is like trying to smell the color nine?" Obviously nine is not a color, and it is impossible to smell a color or a number. I love this phrase because it perfectly explains the difficulty in trying to understand others. And, why do you think you have to? You don't have their experiences or their perspective, so why is it not okay for them to be who they are when you want so much for people to accept *you* for who *you* are?

Many words in our language have different meanings for different people. "Faith," to some, simply means having a belief in GOD. To me, FAITH means having complete TRUST, as I have described before. "Surrender," to some, shows a weakness. "Surrender," to me, shows strength. "Love" is another word that is completely relative based on the person's perception, and the definition is totally subjective to that person's experiences. Your definition of love at age fifteen is likely different than your definition of love at age twenty-five and even at fifty-five. Your definition of love could be completely different from someone who has been abused as a child. It does not mean that they do not love to the best of his/her ability. If someone does not show you that they love you based on *your* definition, that does not mean they do not love you the best they know how. It could be that his/her definition is just different than yours.

You do not have to agree with others' actions, but when you become aware of the times when you see yourself as a victim of their actions, you become aware of another opportunity to learn lessons and to HEAL. Are you a victim of the situation, or is it an opportunity learn lessons and to HEAL?

Does life happen to you, or does life happen for You?

Only the ego makes things personal. If people do things *to* you, you're the one who makes it personal. Not only was it not necessarily their intention, it might not have anything to do with you at all. Your encounter with them is a divine opportunity on your Spiritual Course™ *for* You to grow spiritually. **Activate all lessons that everyone is to learn from this situation or person. Transform all Sources of thinking that life happens *to* you to Unconditional Love & Unconditional Gratitude**™; and **activate all Sources** of knowing that life happens *for* You.

Unfortunately, society promotes this victim way of thinking. Advertisements are all over the television, radio, and billboards for attorneys ready to sue a person or a company that has done something *to* you. If schools try to enforce rules, they risk being sued by an angry parent. If you take a prescription that ends up harming you, fault is placed on the pharmaceutical company. If you choose to smoke and get cancer, blame is placed on the tobacco company. If someone is fired from their job, it is generally the boss's or the company's fault. All these scenarios make you the victim. The victim perspective thinks that everything is someone else's fault or responsibility.

> *When you're a victim,*
> *it is impossible to take action*
> *because you get caught up in the re-action.*

As long as you perceive yourself as a victim, there will always be more opportunities to learn spiritual lessons and to HEAL. When you recognize that you're viewing life from a victim viewpoint, try to look beyond the fear, sadness, disappointment, and anger, and you just may see the TRUTH that you're right where you're supposed to be, experiencing exactly what you need to experience to grow spiritually. If you do not like where you are, **activate all lessons** and **HEAL**!

Being a victim is solely based on your perception of the situation. "Bad" experiences, traumatic memories, and stress all come from a victim perspective, from the viewpoint that life has happened *to* you. You now have the tools and can HEAL at any moment. Note, however, that you don't force a change in your perception because that doesn't alter what you really think and how you really feel. In fact, it is actually a denial of what you really think and feel. You HEAL your perception by **activating all lessons** and **transforming all Sources of feeling like you're a victim of life to Unconditional Love & Unconditional Gratitude™**.

Because we do not have the same experiences, it is impossible for everyone to have the same viewpoints, yet society tries to make everyone conform to a certain set of beliefs. For example, many laws are a way of forcing others to comply with a certain group's belief system. Why can't everyone be allowed to believe the way they do without judgment? The answer is ego. Ego makes people think that their beliefs and ways of doing things are better than others'.

> *We want everyone to think just like us,*
> *yet it is our uniqueness and individuality*
> *that make our world so awesome!*

No one is *ever* better than or not-as-good-as anyone else. The value of a person does not come from how much money you have or don't have, how big of a house you live in or if you don't live in a house at all, what kind of a job you have or don't have, or whether or not you have a college degree. Spiritually speaking, *everyone* is worth the same, and that worth is more valuable than you can ever imagine. Bottom line—it is the value of your Spirit that is the most important!

Life is NOT a competition!

Know that everyone is *always* the best they can be *at the time,* including you. That "best" depends on many factors, including past experiences, the situation, and the mental and emotional state of the person at the time. If they could have done better, they would have. The same goes for you. If you could have done better in a situation, you would have. Sometimes people do things that do not seem that smart—sometimes you do things that don't seem that smart to others. It may or may not be logical; it may or may not make sense. It does not mean they aren't doing their best, and it does not mean that you're not doing your best.

> *There is never a need*
> *to take credit or place blame.*
> *Only the ego takes credit;*
> *only victims place blame.*

115

You are human. That means you're not always perfect, you may sometimes take life personally, you may have negative thoughts, you may feel lower-level emotions, and you have lessons to learn. *But being human is meant to be a wonderful experience.* It is okay to be human, and it is okay to think whatever you think and feel whatever you feel. The key is to become aware of those opportunities to learn lessons and to HEAL all Sources of those lower-level thoughts and emotions.

Life is an opportunity to HEAL!

INFINITE HEALING™ PRINCIPLE #8: YOU ATTRACT WHAT YOU LIVE

The Law of Attraction is in affect *all the time*, every fraction of every second, every second of every minute, every minute of every hour, every hour of every day, every day of every week, every week of every month—well, you get the point—regardless of what you're doing. Because energy follows thought and because you're *continually* having thoughts, energy *continually* follows your thoughts, which means that you *continually* **attract what you live!**

Most techniques associated with the Law of Attraction are based on the principle of affirmations, which are very powerful, and although many have seen tremendous results using them, others have become discouraged because they do not work for them. Affirmations *are* setting the energy the way you want it (IH Tool #4). They attract the energy you want while you're doing the affirmations and sometimes for a while after. But if you doubt the affirmation somewhere in your Mind—if you feel like you're lying to yourself while stating the affirmations—the affirmations are not doing what you want them to, guaranteed. And, if you live the opposite of what you affirm, you ultimately attract the opposite of what you want more often than you attract what you affirmed. Remember, it is the **thought** and the **emotion** attached to the thought that attracts the energy. The stronger the emotion attached to the thought, the stronger and faster the attraction of the energy. Are the emotions attached to your affirmations as strong as the fear (or other negative emotion) that you feel in your daily life?

As an example, let's say you take time daily to state your affirmations. You state over and over that you're financially abundant. During this time, you visualize exactly what you want your house to look like, your car, your clothes, and even your life. You try to *see* yourself living in financial abundance. You try to *know* what it feels like to live in *that* life. You try to *feel* like you're actually living that life. Affirmation time is over, and now it is time to get back to life.

In your current reality, you know that the money going out is more than the money coming in. You fear that there may not be enough money to pay the bills when they are due. You know that you "cannot afford" a new car. You know with the "economy the way it is" that you cannot sell your house because you owe more than it is worth. If car or appliance troubles appear, you fear that the outcome will be more than you can "afford." You dread balancing the checkbook or checking your account balance for fear of what you might see. You basically *live* in financial fear 90+% of the time. Even if you affirmed that you're financially abundant 10% of the time, you're still attracting financial deficiency more often than you're trying to attract financial abundance.

If you *live* the opposite of what you affirm, you'll attract the opposite of what you want most of the time because **you continually attract what you live.** Can you attach as strong of an emotion to your affirmations of financial abundance as you have the fear of financial deficiency? Even if you can, will the time you spend on affirmations override the 90+% of the time that you live and feel the fear of financial deficiency?

Affirmations do not get rid of fear or any other lower-level belief or emotion. They attempt to create a new belief or override (suppress, deny or ignore) the fear or other lower-level belief or emotion. You can attract what you want sooner by becoming aware of what you're attracting by how you *live*. Affirmations—setting the energy the way you want it—are much more effective when you can HEAL the Sources of the lower-level beliefs and emotions that create what you don't want.

Have you ever felt fear so strong that it inhibits your ability to function? Have you ever felt GRATITUDE so strong that it fills your heart so fully that it feels like your physical Body is not big enough to hold it? Can you make the feeling behind your affirmations as strong as the fear you feel if you don't have or get what you want? Can you attach a strong, positive emotion to an affirmation if you do not "feel" it? How do you know what it feels like to be financially abundant if you've never been financially abundant? How do you know what it feels like to feel Joy if you've never felt Joy? How do you know what it feels like to have what you want if you've never had it?

With Infinite Healing™, you do not need to know all that. Use the Infinite Healing™ tools to learn all lessons that everyone is to learn from you being financially deficient and HEAL what you're living that is creating that deficiency. Then activate all Sources that create what you want.

"I activate all Sources that create my financial abundance."

Because you attract what you live, it is very important in HEALING your life that you're conscious of your thoughts. This gives you insight as to why you attract certain things in your life—your HEALTH, your relationships, your jobs, your finances, etc. Are you one of those who go through life on auto-pilot, taking it as it comes, leaving life to chance, reacting instead of acting, without the consciousness that you have created what you have *and* what you don't have, without the consciousness that you *can* create something different, but in order to do so, you must learn the lessons you're to learn from your current situation and HEAL what is attracting what you don't want?

If you do not consciously navigate your life, you're choosing to live on auto-pilot; just like not making a decision is actually to decide (not to decide) and *not* to take action really *is* taking action (to do nothing). Are you playing the leading role in your life, or are you just one of the extras?

Because you attract what you live, complaining attracts more of what you complain about. Fear attracts more of what you fear. Judgment attracts more judgment. LOVE attracts more LOVE, and GRATITUDE attracts more of what you're grateful for.

Stacie Farnham

> *You attract what you live.*
> *What are you living that is*
> *attracting things you don't want?*

> *Infinite Healing*™
> *is more than abundant thinking;*
> *Infinite Healing*™ *is abundant* **living!**

INFINITE HEALING™ PRINCIPLE #9: IT *IS* WHAT IT *IS*

It Is What It Is means that you surrender how you think it "should" be and accept what has happened for what it *Is*—an opportunity. Remember that your life is divinely orchestrated *for* You and that absolutely *everything* that happens in your life is either a blessing or an opportunity to learn lessons and to HEAL.

It Is What It Is means that you accept your experiences as experiences and that you HONOR what you really think and what you really feel. If your experience triggers anger, it triggers anger. *It Is what it Is.* Become aware that it is an opportunity to learn lessons and to HEAL and do it! If you take life personally during an experience, you take life personally. *It Is what it Is.* HONOR the way you really feel, learn the lessons, and HEAL the anger (and everything else you're feeling)! If you're hurt by the comment of another, you're hurt. *It Is what it Is.* HONOR that it hurt you, **activate all lessons** and HEAL **the hurt** (and everything else you're feeling)! HONOR You, **learn the lessons,** and HEAL!

You are human, and one of the greatest things about being human is your ability to *feel* emotion. When you judge what you think or what you feel, you think lower-level thoughts about yourself, so you suppress, deny, and ignore what you feel, and in the process, you fail to HONOR You. Then negative energy settles into the physical and creates dis-ease in your Body and in your life.

It Is What It Is does not mean that you're detached or apathetic about your experiences. It does not mean that you should not have any thoughts or emotions associated with the experience. Becoming detached or apathetic suppresses, denies, or ignores what you really think and what you really feel. You should never get to a point where you don't care about anything, where you're numb to life. Not allowing thoughts or emotions associated with any experience suppresses, denies and ignores You. If you do not allow yourself to feel sadness, sorrow, or hurt, you also filter yourself from feeling happiness, Love and Joy.

When I refer to happiness, Love, or Joy, I mean feeling True happiness, True Love, or True Joy. There is a big difference between love and feeling True unconditional Love, happiness and True happiness, joy and True Joy. True high-level feelings make you smile just because. They fill your heart and your chest cavity to a point where it feels like you can't expand any further, to a point where you don't feel like you can breathe in any more, yet there is no need to. May you Heal yourself to a point where you can experience these True feelings that I am talking about.

Honor who You are by accepting that *It Is What It Is.*

It Is What It Is
I think what I think
I feel what I feel
I Am who I Am
I accept Me
Then I Heal all negative energy that
I don't want by
activating all lessons and transforming all Sources to
Unconditional Love & Unconditional Gratitude™

Be careful not to make your experiences into something they do not have to be. Because you often instinctively base your current perceptions on past or learned experiences, there may be times when you instinctively make situations into something other than what they could Be. When you become aware of those times when you do this, you can take the opportunity to learn lessons and to Heal, which changes your instinctive reaction.

Everything that happens on your Spiritual Course™ is *for* You. Stressing about running late does not get you there on time. Being angry about missing a plane does not put you on that plane. Wishing things had turned out differently does not mean they turned out differently. Let your life be what it Is. If you're stressing about running late, **activate all lessons** and HEAL all Sources of the fear of being late. If you're angry about missing a plane, **activate all lessons** and HEAL all Sources of the anger, and if you're disappointed in the outcome of a situation, **activate all lessons** and HEAL all Sources of the disappointment. Let it be what it Is and HEAL it while you're in it. Maybe that extra few seconds you had to wait was just enough time for you to avoid being in an accident, and maybe missing the plane prevented you from being somewhere else that may have had a disastrous outcome. Even though you may not always know the "why," whatever you encounter in life is exactly what you're supposed to be experiencing at the time.

It Is What It Is. If it was supposed to be something different, it would have been different. If it appears on your Spiritual Course™, it is there *for* You. Surrender how you think it "should" be by accepting what it Is and HEALING when the opportunities present themselves.

Infinite Healing™ Principle #10: *You MUST Honor YOU to Truly HEAL*

This concept has been reiterated many times thus far, but it is so important that it is actually the last of the principles. In order to Truly Heal, you *must* learn to Honor everything about yourself, learn the spiritual lessons you're meant to learn, and learn to Heal all lower-level thoughts, emotions, and situations in your life, ideally *when you're in it.* Your Spirit soars when you Honor You and then your Mind, Heart, and Body instinctively follow.

+ Denying that you have a negative thought does NOT Honor You (*nor does it negate the energy of that thought*).
+ Ignoring your negative thoughts does NOT Honor You (*nor does it change the fact that you have negative thoughts*).
+ Pretending you do not have negative thoughts does NOT Honor You (*nor does it make you think more positive thoughts*).
+ Forcing positive thoughts does NOT Honor You (*nor does it Heal the negative thoughts*).
+ Ignoring how you feel or pretending that you don't feel the way you do is NOT Honoring You (*nor does it negate the energy of the negative feelings*).
+ Telling yourself that you shouldn't feel sad, hurt, angry, etc. is NOT Honoring You (*nor does it change the fact that you're sad, hurt, angry, etc.*).
+ Trying not to be angry, sad, disappointed, or hurt when you really feel angry, sad, disappointed or hurt is NOT Honoring You (*nor does it change the way you really feel*).
+ Forcing positive emotions or trying to make yourself feel something positive when you really feel something negative denies, ignores, or suppresses the negative and does NOT Honor You (*nor does it change the negative into a positive*).
+ Denying that you're angry with someone, that you're hurt, or that you feel any negative emotion is NOT Honoring

You (*nor does it change that fact that what they did made you angry, hurt, etc.*).

+ Hoping or waiting for the feeling to "go away" is NOT HONORING you (*nor does it make it go away*). Time does not HEAL; you just keep suppressing, denying, and ignoring what you're really feeling, sending it deeper and deeper into your energy, and it continues to wear on your Spirit, Mind, Heart, and Body.

+ Sacrificing who you are to "prevent" lower-level emotions in someone else is NOT HONORING YOU.

+ Being afraid to feel or not wanting to feel is NOT HONORING YOU (*nor does it make you feel* TRULY *happy, joyful, at peace, grateful, etc.*).

Stop trying to apply logic to your thoughts and your feelings. They do not always make sense, and *that's okay!* You should never *not* think a thought and you should never *not* feel a certain way.

If you think it, HONOR it. If you HONOR the thought and don't like it, HEAL it!

If you feel it, HONOR it. If you HONOR it and you don't like the feeling, HEAL it!

If you don't like things in your life, HEAL them!

Learn to be free to be You. Not who you think you should be, not who others think you should be, and certainly not what you think others want you to be. When you try to be someone you're not, you get confused about whom you really *are*. When you try to be someone for anyone else, you're often misguided because who you think they want you to be may not really be who they want you to be. When you are You *for* You, you're always the same person, regardless of who you're around.

Be You for You!

Learn to Trust in You. Trust in God, in the Universe. You are from God, and *everything* from God is Amazing. Therefore, You can be nothing but Amazing! Not in an egotistical you-are-better-than-someone else or someone-else-is-lesser-than-you sort of way, but in a Truly spiritual awesome, Amazing way. You may have heard that before. You may have even said that to yourself before. But do you BELIEVE it, without a doubt?

If you tie your self-worth to your job, your belongings, other people's opinions, old beliefs, the past, your thoughts, your feelings, or the outcome of a performance or a game, you're dis-HONORING You. All of those things are ego-based and none of them TRULY define who You really *are*. Even who You are now has nothing to do with your self-worth. If you do allow any of those things to define your self-worth, you have lessons to learn and opportunities to HEAL. Remember, *everyone* is worth the same, and that worth is more valuable than you can ever imagine. Use the Infinite Healing™ tools to HEAL ego-based beliefs and dare to experience the power of...You!

> **"I activate all lessons
> that everyone is to learn from all experiences
> that have created low self-worth."**
> **"I transform all Sources
> of attaching my self-worth to the job I have to
> Unconditional Love & Unconditional Gratitude™."**
> **"I transform all Sources
> of defining my self-worth to what I have to
> Unconditional Love & Unconditional Gratitude™."**
> **"I transform all Sources of relating
> my self-worth to what other people think of me to
> Unconditional Love & Unconditional Gratitude™."**
> **"I activate all Sources
> that allow me to be free to be ME!"**
> **"I activate all Sources
> that create me to realize the TRUE value of ME!"**

If you do not HONOR *everything* about yourself, including everything you think or have thought and everything you feel or have felt, you're refusing to accept who You are now. This dis-HONORS your Spirit and makes it impossible to TRULY HEAL.

Think what you think, learn the lessons, and HEAL all thoughts you don't want. Feel what you feel, learn the lessons, and HEAL the

Sources of all emotions you don't like to feel. Become aware of the HEALING opportunities that life presents to you and HEAL them! When you become aware of whom YOU are now and take advantage of the opportunities to learn lessons and to HEAL, you'll discover not only how amazing YOU really are, but how amazing everyone else in the world is as well.

> *What if you do not become*
> *what you think you should or*
> *what someone else thinks you should?*
> *Then you may just become*
> *who YOU are supposed to BE!*

Additional Infinite Healing™ Tools

Beyond the six basic Infinite Healing™ tools, there are more tools for you to use to HEAL your life. Note that some of these tools may work better for you than others, and some may work better for others than for you. The effectiveness of these tools is based on your perception of your situation. If a tool does not appear to work or you feel like you're trying to force results, try a different tool.

+ Nourish You
+ Get out of your way!
+ Assess what beliefs support your desires
+ Do not carry burdens
+ Nothing has happened
+ Replay events in your Mind
+ Allow yourself to HEAL
+ Change your perspective of time
+ EnJoy your Journey
+ Create your Life Vision
+ Transform you, Transform the world, Transform the Universe
+ Activate your Transformational Mist™

Nourish YOU

Nourishing You, Spirit, Mind, Heart, and Body, is a very important part of Healing at all levels. Helping others, doing things for others, taking care of others, etc. makes you feel good, makes you feel needed, and makes you feel wanted. It is like filling a bag with water. When you do something for others because you *want* to, it adds water to your bag.

Neglecting yourself, putting yourself last, and doing things for others out of obligation or "because you have to" puts holes in your bag. In this analogy, it does not matter how much you water you put in—if you do not fill the holes, your bag can *never* accumulate water. It is like a never-ending task.

Doing things for yourself fills the holes in your bag as if they were never there. It is important that you take time to do something for yourself!

> *How often do you do something FOR yourself*
> *for no reason other than it is FOR you?*

Here are some ideas to give each its own special attention. Nourish your Spirit by applying the Infinite Healing™ tools, by learning the spiritual lessons you're here to learn, with regular meditation and prayer, and most importantly, by having complete Trust in the Universe, in God. Having complete Trust is a *knowing* that everything that happens is *for* You and is *always* in your best spiritual interest, that everything that happens in others' lives is *for* them and is *always* in their best spiritual interest, is being Grateful in advance, is Trusting that God is *always* there *for* You no matter what you're going through, and is Trusting that God, the Universe, knows what is best for You.

Nourish your Mind by nourishing your Spirit, by applying the Infinite Healing™ tools, by Honoring the negative thoughts you have, and transforming all Sources of those thoughts to Unconditional

Love & Unconditional Gratitude™, by removing limits, by making decisions from your Spirit, by being honest with yourself, and by believing in You. Reading positive words also nourish your Mind.

Nourish your Heart by nourishing your Spirit and your Mind, by applying the Infinite Healing™ tools, by Honoring the negative emotions you feel and Healing all Sources as they arise, by doing things that create positivity in your life, by giving and receiving Love, by helping others, by sharing, by laughing, and by doing things you enjoy—for You. (*Doing things out of obligation is much different than doing things out of Love, whether it is for others or for You.*)

Nourish your Body by nourishing your Spirit, your Mind, and your Heart, by applying the Infinite Healing™ tools, with regular exercise, with your choice of quality foods and drink, with alkaline water, with sunshine (in moderation), with quality sleep, and with deep breathing.

Every choice you make, whether it is an action or a reaction, will affect all of You, positively or negatively. Take time to nourish all of You—Spirit, Mind, Heart, and Body.

GET OUT OF YOUR WAY!

One of the main reasons people do not get the results they want with Infinite Healing™ is that they are in their own way and they are limiting their HEALING with their thoughts, beliefs, judgments, etc. Sometimes it is difficult to see where we are in our way, but just because we can't see it does not mean that it is not TRUE. Ever heard the saying, "You are your own worst enemy"? Sometimes you really are.

You have probably heard that it is not your place to judge others. But how often have you heard that it is not your place to judge yourself? Judgment of yourself is one of the main ways you can get in your way. HONORING who you are now, even if you do not like what you're HONORING, is essential to TRUE HEALING and allowing the TRUE YOU to be revealed. HEALING all judgment, toward others and toward YOU, is a very important step in HEALING.

"I transform all Sources
of judgment of myself and others to
Unconditional Love & Unconditional Gratitude™."

You are only able to HEAL to the level that
you're willing to be honest with yourself about
what you really think, what you really feel,
and who you are now.

If you're not willing to be honest about what you really think, you will not be able to HEAL the negative thoughts. If you're not willing to be honest about how you really feel, you suppress, deny, or ignore the lower-level emotions. If you're not willing to be honest with yourself about what happened in the past, you'll not be able to HEAL the past, and you'll carry the trauma with you through your present and into the future. If you're not willing to be honest about who you are now, you'll never allow the TRUE YOU to emerge. Get out of your way by HONORING YOU!

Many people have gotten so good at suppressing, denying, or ignoring what they really think or what they really feel that they do it without knowing they are doing it. They may have convinced themselves for so long that they think a certain way or that they do not feel a certain way that it is sometimes a challenge to become aware of what they *really* think or feel and see the TRUTH. If you're not aware of it, you cannot HONOR it. If you cannot HONOR it, you cannot HEAL it.

It is *always* okay to think what you really think, to feel what you really feel, and to be who you really are. Just make sure that you **activate all lessons** and HEAL the negative things that interfere with your life being *everything* you want it to be.

It Is What It Is is not only an Infinite Healing™ principle; it is also part of getting out of your own way. *It Is What It Is* does *not* mean that since you cannot do anything about what happened, you should ignore what you're really thinking and really feeling about the situation. Besides, you *can* do something about it! You can take advantage of the opportunity to learn lessons and to HEAL!

Navigate your life by telling the Universe what you want and then TRUST that GOD, the Universe knows what is best *for* YOU. If you do not get what you want, it was not meant to be that way at that time. When you force life in a certain direction, the things that will appear on your Spiritual Course™ to get you back on track may be significantly different than what they would have been if you had been willing to flow *with* life. **Get out of your way by navigating your life,** not trying to control it.

ASSESS WHAT BELIEFS SUPPORT YOUR DESIRES

As we discussed in Infinite Healing™ Principle #6, What Your Mind Believes Creates Your Reality, many of your beliefs, whether you're aware of them or not, create limitations in your life. You are the only one who can limit yourself, and you're the only one who can remove those limits. You limit yourself when you try to make everything make sense. You limit yourself by being practical. You limit yourself by having an attachment to the outcome, and you limit yourself by staying within your comfort zone.

Become aware of what You believe and of what beliefs you have accepted from others. Then assess which of those beliefs, if any, are creating the things that you want in your life and which of those are creating things that you do not want in your life. If they support what you want, keep them. If they do not, **activate all lessons everyone is to learn from those beliefs** and **transform all Sources of them to Unconditional Love & Unconditional Gratitude**™.

+ What *do* you believe about life?
  o Life is hard.
  o Life is not fair.
+ What do you believe about genetic or hereditary dis-eases?
  o It runs in my family so it is likely I will get ...
  o My grandmother/grandmother/mother/father had it so I will probably get it.
+ Do you believe that there are limitations in your life—physically or otherwise—"since the accident"?
  o My life went downhill when ...
  o I can't do that since ...
  o My neck always hurts since ...
+ What do you believe about people?
  o People are not nice.
  o People cannot be trusted.

+ What do you believe about your Health?
    o I have (*insert diagnosis here*). i.e. diabetes, COPD, allergies, heart condition, the flu, a bad knee.
    o My allergies act up every spring.
    o I usually get sick during cold and flu season.
+ What do you believe about your weight?
    o I am overweight. I am underweight.
    o I can't lose weight. I can't gain weight.
    o Do you believe that your weight is tied to the foods you eat?
    o Do you believe that certain foods are bad for you?
    o I can't lose weight if I don't exercise, but I do not like to exercise. Exercise is not fun.
+ What do you believe about relationships?
    o Relationships are hard.
    o I never find the right guy (girl).
    o The good ones are already taken.
+ What do you believe about your job?
    o I do not like my job. I hate my job.
    o I am underappreciated.
    o I'm only there for the money.
+ What do you believe about your income?
    o I never make enough to cover the bills.
    o They will never pay me as much as I'm worth.
+ What do you believe about money?
    o I have no money. I never have enough money.
    o It is spent before it comes in.
    o I live paycheck-to-paycheck.
    o I can't afford ...
+ What do you believe about your intelligence?
    o I am not smart. I do not learn easily.
    o I am smarter than most other people.
+ What do you believe about YOU?
    o I can't make friends.

- ○ I'm always late. I can't seem to be on time.
- ○ I don't sleep well. I always wake up in the night.
- ○ I am not good enough.

Do you believe it? Remember, whatever You believe IS true for You! Whatever You believe is what you attract. Whatever You believe is what you communicate to the Universe how it is supposed to be. If you're not aware of the beliefs in your life that interfere with you creating the life you want, you'll not be able to HEAL those interferences. If you're not aware of your beliefs that limit your possibilities and experiences, you're not able to HEAL them. If you're not able to HEAL them, they continue to create a reality that you do not want. This is a key part of HEALING—not only your physical Body, but your life.

Dreams come true faster
when you become aware of
the beliefs and limitations
that are interfering with you achieving them,
you activate all lessons everyone is
to learn from those beliefs and limitations,
and then you HEAL them!

Do Not Carry Burdens

As our days are filled with life's responsibilities, we sometimes get overwhelmed trying to fit it all in—work, children, spouse, family, school, housework, dinner, extracurricular activities, etc. We feel like we don't have time to nourish ourselves or to do things for *us* because there is so much to do. Stress builds up and causes more stress, and life becomes a burden. This creates even more stress and more burdens, which in turn create energy that is chaotic. Remember that chaos on the inside creates chaos on the outside, and chaos attracts chaos.

Stress is human-created and is detrimental to the condition of your WHOLE being. Stress is mental and is created only in your Mind, by your *perception of the situation*. It is conceived from having an attachment to the outcome, from wanting the outcome to be a certain way and/or *fearing* that it might not turn out the way you want or think it should. Stress is the effect of thinking that you might know what is better for you than GOD, the Universe, does.

Become aware of when you're carrying burdens, whether they are yours or someone else's.

"Look at what you've done to me."

"Because of you, I feel ..."

"Because of you, I am ..."

"Because of you, I ..."

"I have to ..."

Activate all lessons and **transform all Sources of guilt or regret or anything else you feel about an action or reaction you had to Unconditional Love & Unconditional Gratitude**™. Guilt and regret are sure signs that you're carrying a burden. Another sure sign is if you have tension across the shoulders. When you become aware that you're carrying burdens, ask yourself, "What is a burden in my life?" If the answer comes easily, **activate all lessons** and **transform all Sources of feeling burdened to Unconditional Love & Unconditional Gratitude**™." If nothing comes to Mind, **activate**

all lessons and **transform all Sources of feeling like life is a burden to Unconditional Love & Unconditional Gratitude™.** The Body does not lie, so even if you cannot make sense of it, HEAL it!

Stress can be reduced and even eliminated when you come to understand that *everything* happens for a reason, and that reason is for you to learn spiritual lessons, whether or not you can make logical sense of what happened and when you understand that everything *always* happens in your best spiritual interest, whether it is to get your attention or to get you refocused on your purpose. If something does not turn out the way you wanted it or the way you thought it should have, you have lessons to learn and opportunities to HEAL. You choose whether to ignore or deny the opportunity or whether to take advantage of it. Regardless of what you choose to do, it happened exactly the way it was meant to happen *for* You.

> *There is no such thing*
> *as a mistake or failure in life.*
> *There are lessons to learn and*
> *opportunities to HEAL.*

Everything you experience, whether you're an active participant or an observer, provides an opportunity for You to make this world a better place.

HEAL the perspective that you "have to" do something so you can now see it as you "get to" do it. HEAL the perspective that you "should" do something so you can now see it as you "can" do it. "I get to go to work" vs "I have to go to work." "I can exercise" vs "I should exercise." The difference in the energy behind the perspective is significant. Doing things out of obligation is *never* from a vibration of Unconditional Love & Unconditional Gratitude™.

Doing things out of obligation not only creates burdens, but it often creates expectations, and expectations that are not met create more burdens. If you're going to do something, do it unconditionally, because you *want* to, not because you feel like you have to, and not because you want something in return. If you're expecting anything in return, even if it is a simple "thank you," you are *not* doing it unconditionally. HEAL obligations and any expectations so you can give unconditionally.

> *You must HEAL the perspective*
> *to free yourself from the burden.*

Life should never, ever be a burden. Life really is meant to be JOYFUL, easily flowing in HARMONY. If it is not, you have lessons to learn and opportunities to HEAL. HEAL the little things that create stress throughout your day so the little things in life do not build up and become a burden.

We tend to be very protective over those we love. If they have stress, we often have stress. If they are encountering lower-level experiences, we worry about them. We sometimes empathize so much with them that we take on their burdens. Remember that they are experiencing exactly what they need on *their* Spiritual Course™ *for* them to grow spiritually. Use the Infinite Healing™ tools to HEAL You so you do not carry their burdens. Encourage them to use the Infinite Healing™ tools to learn their lessons and to HEAL their situation.

> *Carrying someone else's burden*
> *does not lighten the load for them!*
> *Worrying about someone else's situation*
> *does not make their situation better.*
> *Distressing about what someone else*
> *is going through*
> *does not fix it for them.*
> *In fact, in all of these situations,*
> *you actually add negative energy*
> *to their situation.*

NOTE: *If a loved one is encountering a lower-level experience and you're aware of it, there is a lesson in it for* You *as well.* **Activate all lessons that everyone is to learn from the situation and transform all Sources to Unconditional Love & Unconditional Gratitude™.** *Use Infinite Healing™ to* HEAL You *and them!*

Do not carry burdens—yours or anyone else's. HEALING allows you to feel compassion for others without carrying the burden. Get out of your way by HEALING the burdens in life! Let the Universe work *for* You, the way it is supposed to be *for* You!

NOTHING HAS HAPPENED

Use this tool for physical trauma. Anything that creates trauma is a less-than-desirable experience, and in all less-than-desirable experiences, the first thing to do is to **activate all lessons that everyone is to learn from that experience.**

If you have a physical injury or physical trauma, immediately **activate all lessons that everyone is to learn from the experience, transform all Sources of everything you're feeling to Unconditional Love & Unconditional Gratitude**™, and **say "Nothing has happened"** over and over.

"Nothing has happened" is not denying what has happened. It is not lying to yourself by trying to convince yourself that nothing has happened because generally the pain of an injury will certainly make you know that something *has* happened.

The intent behind this tool is simply to tell the physical cells not to store any trauma and they should continue to vibrate as if nothing happened. It prevents trauma from storing in the physical Body by HEALING the trauma instantly.

However, if you do feel like you're lying to yourself by using this tool, it is *not* going to be effective. It is the belief and intent behind it that makes it work or not work. If you're saying "nothing has happened" but you're thinking that something did *too* happen, you will not be able to impact the physical cells as intended.

It also has much more amazing results if there is no fear or other lower-level perceptions associated with the event. Injury often triggers fear, anger, disappointment, and a variety of other lower-level emotions. Negative emotions will interfere with the possibility of the trauma HEALING instantly. If you're aware that there is fear or anger or disappointment or any other lower-level feelings, **transform all Sources of them to Unconditional Love & Unconditional Gratitude**™ and then use **"nothing has happened."**

I have used this tool many, many times with tremendous results. I have also heard numerous testimonials of how this has helped others.

This tool has been effective in moving broken bones and in reducing and preventing pain, inflammation, and bruising. Remember the story of when I broke my ankle? This situation provided me the most amazing experience I have had with this tool. As I lay there, I saw that my foot was not pointing in the right direction. I immediately started saying in my head, "nothing has happened" over and over with my full concentration on my foot. As I said this, I saw my foot move as if in slow motion as it set back to the place where it was supposed to be. Although it seemed to me that it was moving slowly, it all happened so fast that I have not found one person who witnessed the slide into home who even noticed the position of my foot before it set back into place. I did not feel any pain as I lay there. In fact, the most pain I experienced at the time was as I was being carried off the field and my ankle bounced with each step. With each bounce, I kept repeating "nothing has happened." Once off the field, they put me in a chair with my leg elevated. There was very little swelling and minimal pain. The firemen arrived and performed their standard test to assess whether or not they thought it was broken. One had me push forward against his hand to test the force and pull my ankle back toward my Body. The final assessment—"in his professional opinion," as he put it—was that it was not broken. The x-rays the next day proved otherwise—complete breaks on both the inside and outside ankle bones, which later required surgery to put them back together.

Because I was in minimal pain and had no fear from the incident, I did not go to the emergency room that night. I went home, worked with the energy the best I knew how at the time, and called the doctor the next morning to schedule an appointment. It was 5:00 pm before they could see me. I rescheduled many of my clients that week, but my sister had an appointment for a Prime Meridian GoldZone™ (via the feet) with me that next day, so I had her keep her session (and she even brought me lunch!). We did have to make some minor adjustments in positioning for me to complete her GoldZone, but there was no reason I could not see her.

"Nothing has happened" was the tool I used the most during my recovery as Infinite Healing™ was in the early stages, and it has evolved so significantly because of this experience. I believe that because I used this tool immediately, the trauma to my physical Body was *minimal!* The ankle/foot had very little inflammation; I had discomfort but no pain, and minimal bruising. Imagine what it would have been like if I had *all* of the Infinite Healing™ tools as they are outlined in this book!

I have used this tool when I've smashed my finger in a drawer, stubbed my toe, ran into a doorjamb with a box, strained a muscle on the softball field, got hit by a softball, and numerous other occasions. I use it when infants, toddlers, or children get hurt. Others have seen scars diminish by "going back to" the event in their Mind and using this tool.

This tool can also be used in the middle of trauma or before impending trauma if you're conscious enough to use it. I use this tool if I see an accident about to occur or in the process of occurring. "Nothing has happened" is a very powerful tool to shift the energy in a positive way. Use this tool with **activating all lessons and transforming all Sources to Unconditional Love & Unconditional Gratitude**™, and you'll receive *very* powerful results!

REPLAY EVENTS IN YOUR MIND

Although you may not be able to undo what has happened, you *can* HEAL the energy of what happened.

Sometimes we replay events in our Mind over and over and over. These are often very JOYOUS occasions or very traumatic situations. Remember, the Mind cannot tell the difference between what is real and what is imagined. If it occurs in the Mind, it is *real* to your energy. *Each time you replay an event in your Mind, you reinforce the energy around that event.* If you replay a happy moment in your life, you may experience the emotions you felt when you were there, and it makes you smile. If you replay a traumatic experience in your life, it triggers the fear, anger, and hurt you experienced when you were there. In either scenario, you're giving energy direction and power *each and every time* you replay it.

So, replay those happy and JOYOUS occasions as many times as you want, but be cautious (and conscious) of how you replay those not-so-desirable situations. When you replay negative events with a negative outcome, remember that you reinforce that negative energy every time. When you replay events from a victim perspective, you reinforce that you were the victim *every time* you play it.

Because you can go to past experiences in your Mind and anything that occurs in your Mind is real, you can HEAL past experiences, often as easily as you can current experiences. HONOR the experience, HONOR what you thought or still think of the experience, and HONOR how you felt and still feel about the experience. Make sure you **activate all lessons that everyone is to learn from that experience** and **transform all Sources of everything you felt and still feel about the experience to Unconditional Love & Unconditional Gratitude™.**

Your Mind creates reference points based on your perceptions of your experiences and the emotions associated with those perceptions. This applies to both positive and negative experiences—those that trigger happiness, JOY, and delight, and those that trigger fear, sadness, hurt, anger, and disappointment. This is how your Mind tries to fit your current experiences into what it *does* know. When something happens that is similar or the same as an event that happened previously, your Mind instinctively refers to that reference point, which activates an instinctive perception and triggers the same or similar emotions. For example, if you were in a car accident at an intersection, you may experience fear or anxiety when you approach or go through that intersection again, or any intersection. This is not because of the current experience—it is because there is trauma remaining from the previous one. If someone surprised you and it was not a pleasant experience, you may tend to not like surprises. On the other hand, if someone surprised you and it was a Joyous experience, you likely enjoy surprises.

To create a new reference point, you must HEAL any trauma that was experienced when the reference point was created. Remember that if negative emotions were triggered, there is trauma associated with that experience. One way to create a new reference point is to replay in your Mind the traumatic experience and first, **activate all lessons that everyone is to learn from that experience**, then **transform all Sources of trauma that you experienced to Unconditional Love & Unconditional Gratitude**™. When the trauma is HEALED, the reference point is HEALED so when you go back in your Mind to that experience, it now seems insignificant. Sometimes when you HEAL trauma and HEAL a reference point, you do not remember the event at all (and if you've activated all lessons, you keep the lesson!).

Another way to create a new reference point is to go back in your Mind to the traumatic experience and first, **activate all** lessons that everyone is to learn from that experience. Then, *with the intent of transforming all Sources of the trauma that you experienced to Unconditional Love & Unconditional Gratitude*™, **replay the event in your Mind from a different view.** One of the great things of replaying it in your Mind is that you get to choose the view from which you "see" the event. For example, maybe you can replay it as if you're watching a movie where you're *not* the victim, but you can see the victim, or you can replay it as if it had a completely different outcome. Make sure you're **activating all lessons** that everyone is to learn from that experience and **transform all Sources of trauma and everything that was felt to Unconditional Love & Unconditional Gratitude**™. When you can easily replay the event without being triggered or you can replay it with a different outcome, you know the trauma has been transformed and HEALED. For example, in the event where I broke my ankle, I would replay it in my Mind as if I had just run through home plate and scored.

This tool does not deny that the event happened. It allows you to HEAL everything around the event from a safe place. However, if you feel like you're lying to yourself by using this tool, it will not be effective. In addition to using the main Infinite Healing™ tools, replaying events is how "bad" memories and past trauma can be HEALED.

If it is a severely traumatic experience, you can replay it from a bystander's perspective rather than from the victim point of view. This is often a safer way to access and HEAL traumatic events. As you HEAL from the observer standpoint, you can eventually HEAL from the victim standpoint without the level of trauma that was originally experienced. The key to remember in any traumatic experience is that there are lessons to learn and opportunities to HEAL. Take advantage of those opportunities so you do not continue to carry the trauma with you through your present and into your future.

Please note that some traumas seem to HEAL easily and other traumas are much too painful. If a tool does not appear to work or you feel like you're forcing results, try a different tool.

ALLOW YOURSELF TO HEAL

Consciously wanting to HEAL or saying the words "I allow myself to HEAL" does not mean you're really allowing yourself to HEAL. Telling yourself that you allow yourself to HEAL does not necessarily mean you're literally allowing yourself to HEAL. Being ready in your logical Mind does not mean that you're actually ready. You have to be ready spiritually, mentally, emotionally, and physically. You must HEAL what is in the way of your HEALING.

If you're holding on to anger, hurt, pain, disappointment, etc. as a "reminder" or a "protection" to prevent "it" from happening again, it *will* continue to impact your life negatively and it *will* be reflected in your physical Body. Keeping any lower-level emotion *will* prevent you from HEALING. You *can* keep the lesson without keeping the trauma. Remember, when you set up protections against emotions, you block yourself from *all* emotions, not just the negative ones. If you do not open yourself to feel hurt, you interfere with you being able to deeply feel LOVE.

It is safe to experience life!

If you're so set in your beliefs that you're unwilling to consider a different perspective, you may be in your way of HEALING. If you're living on auto-pilot, you're not allowing yourself to HEAL. If your life is not abundant, there is something keeping you from HEALING. If you're not enjoying life, there are limitations in your HEALING. If you judge yourself for your thoughts or your feelings, you'll never TRULY allow yourself to HEAL.

What you may perceive as your weaknesses may actually be clues to reveal your greatest strengths, and discovering these often uncovers gifts and your TRUE SELF. Give yourself permission to be open to other perspectives and new experiences, to believe differently, to be conscious of life, to be abundant, to really ENJOY life, to think the way you think, to feel the way you feel, to be YOU without judgment, and to Truly Heal. What you may initially perceive as being crazy may not be as crazy as you think.

Why would you stay in the way of Truly Healing when you have the tools to get out of your way? Why would you keep the trauma, especially when it is so easy to Heal with the tools you now have? It is time to experience a whole new way of Healing!

**"I activate all Sources
that create True Healing in Me!"**

Change Your Perspective of Time

According to Albert Einstein's Law of Relativity, there is no time, nor space. Time is human-made, and we have created linear time with our clocks and calendars. This is how we have become accustomed to measuring time, to planning our day, to organizing our lives. We *live* according to linear time.

Linear time actually assigns limits to our conscious thinking and is relative to each person's perception. For one person, a ride home took "forever." For another travelling in the same vehicle, it was quick. Because time is relative to each person's perception, time can be flexible. Because time in *your* life is relative to *your* perception, you can make time more versatile to work *for* You.

> *When you need more time, slow down time;*
> *when you're in a situation*
> *when you want time to go faster,*
> *speed up time.*
> *It really IS that simple.*

This tool is actually another way of implementing Infinite Healing™ Tool #4, where you navigate your life the way you want it. You can set the energy the way you want it—**"Slow down time to allow me to get to my destination by 4:00,"** or you can activate all Sources that create what you want—**"I activate all Sources that create me arriving at my destination by 4:00."**

If I am running late, I slow down time and set the energy that I will arrive at my destination by a certain time on my car clock. Then I free myself from the attachment to the outcome and have complete Trust that I will arrive exactly when I am supposed to.

I have found that if I stress that I am going to be late, I fuel the energy that I'm going to be late, and most often times I *am* late. When I slow down time, set the energy the way I want it, and have complete Trust that it will be exactly as it is supposed to be *for* me, most often,

I arrive early or right on time. If I do arrive late, I understand that I was supposed to be late even if I do not understand why.

Note that when I slow down time, I do not look at the clock. Looking at the clock puts my logical-thinking Mind into a panic that I am going to be late, which causes stress, which fuel the energy that I am going to be late, which makes me late.

You have certain beliefs of how much time it takes to get from point A to point B. You add in extra time in high traffic. You logically plan your life around time. But in order to allow time to be flexible, you must HEAL those expectations.

As I have said many times, energy does not always make sense to the human Mind. As I have experimented with changing my perspective of time, I have made it from point A to point B in ten minutes, a trip that traditionally took me thirty minutes. Winter used to seem like forever and summer seemed to rush by, whereas now, winter goes by in a perfect amount of time and my summers seem longer.

Did you hear as a youngster that the older you get, the faster time goes? Even though you may not have been able to fathom that then, did you store that belief somewhere inside and now as the years pass, does it really go faster? Is that because there is a belief system in place?

Slow down time, detach yourself from the outcome, and TRUST *that you'll arrive at the exact time you're supposed to* for YOU. If you do not arrive when you wanted and it triggers negative emotions, **activate all lessons you are to learn from being late** and **transform all Sources of everything you're feeling to Unconditional Love & Unconditional Gratitude**™.

If I am in a situation where I really don't want to be there, I speed up time. Time seems to go faster, and even though the clock says I am getting out at a certain time, it did not seem to drag by. Please note that I rarely use this tool anymore because I do not ever *have* to be somewhere I don't want to be, and I have learned to enjoy my journey.

This concept gives whole new meaning to time management. ☺

EnJOY Your Journey

Life is not supposed to be hard so if life is a struggle, you have opportunities to HEAL. Are you taking advantage of them?

Since your past is anything before this moment, your present quickly becomes your past. Everything that you suppress, deny, or ignore keeps you stuck in the trauma of the negative experiences of the past, including regret, guilt, shame, anger, bitterness, hurt, resentment, disappointment, etc. whether the past was an hour ago, yesterday, or years ago. Pretending it is not there does not HEAL the trauma. Ignoring that it happened doesn't HEAL it, nor does wishing it hadn't happened. Denying how you really feel/felt about it doesn't HEAL it. Forcing it out of your Mind or keeping your Mind occupied on other things so you don't have to think about it does not HEAL it. As long as it is there, it will continue to negatively impact your life, now and in the future.

Your life does *not* have to be defined by your past experiences. You may not be able to change your past, but you can certainly HEAL your past! Become aware of what you have stuffed inside, ignored, or pretended like it's not there. **Activate all lessons that everyone is to learn from those experiences** and then **HEAL** it!

Worry and fear about your future create a worrisome and fearful future. Life is a journey, but it does not *have* to be a challenge. Remember that, among other things, it is your actions and reactions that influence what appears next on your Spiritual Course™, and that everything you experience on your Spiritual Course™ is always the right journey *for* You to advance your Spirit. As you learn lessons and HEAL the past, your present becomes much more enjoyable.

Needing to know what is at the destination or which direction you have to take to get where you think you need to be creates stress and burdens, and interferes with you being able to enjoy life. TRUST that you're exactly where you need to be, and that you're experiencing exactly what you need to experience. Learn the lessons you are to learn, HEAL the things in your life you don't like, and make a conscious effort to enjoy *your* journey!

**"I activate all Sources
that create more JOY in my life."**

*Doing things that you enjoy
makes your Spirit smile!*

CREATE YOUR LIFE VISION

Have you ever thought about what you *really* want from life? Do you use affirmations to try to create what you want? Or do you just hope that you get what you think you want? Have you ever told the Universe what you want and made a conscious effort to HEAL what is getting in the way of you already having it?

Your Life Vision is the perfect picture of what you want in your life. It tells the Universe what you want and helps you become aware of why you may not already have it.

Your Life Vision is about the things that inspire and support *your* PURPOSE for being here, like Unconditional LOVE, Unconditional GRATITUDE, TRUST, HARMONY, INTEGRITY, HONESTY, PEACE, JOY, FAITH—just to name a few. When you have these things in your life, you spiritually grow faster in less time. You create abundance in *everything,* and the material things you desire are more easily attainable.

It is unlike a traditional vision board because it goes beyond the material things, like what kind of house you want to live in or what kind of car you want to drive. Planning for material things creates an attachment to the outcome, which can trigger negative thoughts and emotions that get in the way of you creating the life you want.

Here is my Life Vision:

Stacie Farnham

My Life Vision

Dear Universe,

This is the perfect picture of what I want in my life. Make them MY reality NOW!

Sincerely, Stacie Farnham

154

You can see that I included financial harmony. This is because it was one of the things in my life that created the most stress. Once I HEALED the fear and other negative feelings associated with financial deficiency, it became much easier to live in complete TRUST. I was then able to get out of the lower-level energy of stress and get out of my way so the other things that support my PURPOSE could appear.

To create your Life Vision, give some in-depth thought about what you want in your life. To receive the best results, be somewhat detailed, but be cautious about being too specific. Specificity can limit what you get. For example, if you're looking for a loving relationship and you specify what you want your mate to look like, you may be limiting the loving relationship you get.

The two items on my Life Vision that I wanted to be more specific were "loving relationships" and "successful business." I itemized what I wanted in a loving relationship with my spouse and also what I desired in my relationships with my daughters. For my spouse I listed friendship, communication, intimacy, HONESTY, INTEGRITY, TRUST, JOY, shared responsibility, laughter, Unconditional LOVE, Unconditional GRATITUDE, romance, passion, and partnership. For my daughters, I included friendship, communication, HONESTY, INTEGRITY, TRUST, JOY, laughter, Unconditional LOVE, and Unconditional GRATITUDE. The vision for my successful business includes INTEGRITY, HONESTY, respect, abundance of students, awareness and understanding of what I have to offer, to provide valuable education and information, and to help others TRULY HEAL—Spirit, Mind, Heart, and Body. I put these details on the back of my Life Vision.

The next step is to determine the things you do not already have and assess what interferes with you having it. If you do not already have what you want, there are lessons to learn and opportunities to HEAL. For example, if you have included financial harmony as part of your Life Vision, assess what interferes with you already being financially abundant. What are your beliefs about money? What are your fears associated with money? What do you believe about people who have money or that do not have money? What beliefs about finances did you learn growing up? What thoughts do you have on a daily basis that attracts financial deficiency?

Specifically planning how you want your life to go can create an attachment to the outcome and create "construction" if things do not go as you wanted. For example, if you say you want to be married by the age of twenty-five, you may create a marriage that is less than ideal so you meet your goal, or you may become disappointed if you're not married by that age. When life does not meet your plan or expectations, lower-level emotions are triggered, like disappointment, frustration, hopelessness, sadness, etc. Make sure to **activate all lessons** and to HEAL the negative that can be associated with your plan.

Once you identify what is interfering with you having what you want, use Infinite Healing™ tools #2 (activate all lessons) and #3 (transform all Sources to Unconditional Love & Unconditional Gratitude™) to HEAL them. When you can become aware of what is in your way you can HEAL at the details and you'll make faster progress.

> **"I activate all lessons that I am to learn from not having _____ in my life.**
> **I transform all Sources that interfere**
> **with my Life Vision being MY reality to**
> **Unconditional Love & Unconditional Gratitude™."**

Now, activate all Sources that create what you want.

> **"I activate all Sources**
> **that infinitely create INTEGRITY in my life."**
> **"I activate all Sources**
> **that infinitely create HARMONY in my life."**
> **"I activate all Sources that infinitely create ME**
> **to see myself and others without judgment."**
> **"I activate all Sources that infinitely create ME**
> **to be TRULY HEALTHY—Spirit, Mind, Heart, and Body."**
> **"I activate all Sources that infinitely create MY**
> **awareness and understanding of my Gifts."**

**"I activate all Sources that infinitely create
loving relationships in my life."**

It is imperative that you TRUST that what happens in your life is always *for* You. If you do not like what has appeared on your Spiritual Course™, HEAL it! If you do not like what life is giving you, learn your lessons and HEAL! You cannot TRUST that what happens in your life is always *for* You if you're a victim of the past.

And lastly, be TRULY GRATEFUL for every step of HEALING and for *every time* you get what you said you wanted.

After you assemble your Life Vision, keep it visible. Look at it every day. Which one stands out as needing to be HEALED today? The more you HEAL the reasons you do not already have what you want and activate all Sources that create your desires, the sooner you may have what you wish for. Navigate your life by creating *your* Life Vision!

TRANSFORM YOU, TRANSFORM THE WORLD, TRANSFORM THE UNIVERSE

You cannot make others change, no matter how hard you try. You cannot force them conform to your beliefs, and you cannot guarantee that they will react the way you think they should. They do not have your experiences, so it is unlikely that they could ever have the exact same perspective as you. So instead of thinking that it is everyone else who needs to be fixed, and instead of trying to fix everyone else, why not start with HEALING YOU?

> *You must HEAL yourself*
> *to change the world.*

Because YOU are a *significant* part of the Universe, when you transform all Sources of *your* lower-level thoughts and emotions to Unconditional Love & Unconditional Gratitude™, you increase the vibration of the energy that is in the Universe and you transform the negative into a positive. This means that there is less anger, frustration, judgment, disappointment, etc. in the world. When you increase the vibration of energy in the Universe, more people come in contact with the higher vibration and will entrain higher. When you use Infinite Healing™ to HEAL YOU, you do HEAL the world, and yes, even the Universe.

You can also transform all Sources of energy you come in contact with to Unconditional Love & Unconditional Gratitude™ even when you're not working on HEALING you. This includes energy you come directly in contact with, energy around people or situations that you hear about, or energy associated with events all the way around the world. With Infinite Healing™, there are no limits.

"I activate all lessons that everyone is to learn from that situation. I transform all Sources of that situation to Unconditional Love & Unconditional Gratitude™."

Be cautious of media. Stories that you hear on television or the radio, or that you read in the newspaper or online, are often relayed from a victim viewpoint, from a perspective of something happening *to* another. Media triggers lower-level instinctive perceptions and emotions, elicits judgment, and triggers anger, disappointment, sadness, sorrow, and especially fear.

You can be educated without being persuaded.

This means you can be aware of what is going on in the world without getting caught up in the chaos and negativity of the incidents that are reported.

Take into consideration terrorist acts, a shooting in a school or a movie theater, bombings at public events, etc. These experiences elicit an enormous amount of judgment, anger, fear, and a wide range of other low-level emotions. The coverage of these events keeps people stuck in the trauma—the anger, the fear, the sorrow, etc.—of what happened. Remember, it is thoughts and emotions that give energy force and direction. When a large number of people are strongly feeling judgment, anger, fear, sorrow, hurt, confusion, etc., the strength of the energy of those low-level feelings is very, very powerful. In taking part in this, you send more of "that" judgment and those lower-level emotions into the situation and to those involved. Remember the concept of resonance and entrainment. When two or more energies come near each other, one of three things will happen. Lower-level energies will entrain to a higher level, one will lower and one will rise, or the higher-level energy will decrease to the lower-level energy. When there is an abundance of such powerfully strong negative thoughts and emotions surrounding a tragic event, it is the third scenario that occurs. Higher-level energies are entrained to the lower-level very quickly. This actually puts *more* judgment, anger, fear, etc. into the Universe.

Remember that *each* and every one of us is on our own Spiritual Course™ and our experiences provide lessons to learn and opportunities to HEAL. Those involved in such catastrophic situations (and everyone else that hears about them) have spiritual lessons to learn. If they were not meant to experience it, they would have been somewhere else. Infusing more sorrow, sadness, pity, anguish, distress, misery, etc. into the experience builds more sorrow, sadness, pity, anguish, distress, and misery in the Universe. Keep in Mind that it is very important that if you think it or feel it that you **HONOR** it, **activate all lessons that everyone is to learn from it**, and **HEAL** it. Use the Infinite Healing™ tools to help HEAL you, HEAL them, and HEAL the Universe. Although it does not change the fact that they were involved in the situation, it may make their experience less negative. The more we can HEAL the lower-level mentality that creates such events, the less these events will happen.

If it were you, would you want negative thoughts and emotions associated with the situation, or would you prefer that Unconditional Love & Unconditional Gratitude™ be affiliated with the situation?

The ones who are hardest to LOVE often need LOVE the most.

The person who committed the violent acts did so because that is what they did. You may *never, ever* be able to understand the perspective the assailant was coming from and it may *never, ever* make sense, no matter how hard you try to understand it. Judgment of that person, anger, bitterness, resentment, hate, rage, etc. toward that person does *not* make this world a better place. Again, if you think it or feel it, HONOR it and HEAL it!

Activating all lessons and transforming all Sources of judgment, anger, bitterness, resentment, hate, rage, etc. toward that person and the situation to Unconditional Love & Unconditional Gratitude™ *does* make this world a better place. What are *you* contributing?

Consider a media fast, or, if you must participate in the news, become aware if you get caught up in the lower-level energy of what they report. Make a conscious effort to incorporate Infinite Healing™

when you hear of or read stories that trigger these typical lower-level tendencies.

> "I activate all lessons
> that everyone is to learn from that experience."
> "I transform all Sources
> of everything that everyone is feeling right now to
> Unconditional Love & Unconditional Gratitude™."
> "I transform all Sources
> of that situation and all of those involved to
> Unconditional Love & Unconditional Gratitude™."
> "I activate all Sources
> that create TRUE HEALING in the world."
> "I activate all Sources
> that allow people to see this situation and
> all of those involved without judgment."

The best thing you can do in any crisis, whether it is your experience or something you hear or read about, is to integrate the Infinite Healing™ tools into your life.

ACTIVATE YOUR TRANSFORMATIONAL MIST™

Some people set up protections around their energy out of fear that it will be invaded or attacked. Fear of having your energy permeated attracts and increases the misfortune of it happening.

An alternative is to activate your Transformational Mist™. It radiates from your Infinite Core* and envelops you, is above you, below you, and on all sides of you. The Mist is within you and you're within the Mist. The concept of the Transformational Mist™ is not to protect you, because when you need protection, it is based in fear. The Mist is about FAITH. It is about the Divine Light of Unconditional Love and Unconditional Gratitude™.

> *Your Infinite Core is an energetic "tube" that lies vertically in the center of You and it extends infinitely above you and infinitely below you. It flows abundantly with the Divine Light.

The Mist can be as close to your physical Body as you want it to be, to the outer edge of your aura, or it can extend as far as you can see or even beyond. The intent of activating your Transformational Mist™ is to transform all energy that you come in contact with or that comes in contact with the Mist to Unconditional Love & Unconditional Gratitude™. This includes every thought, every emotion, the energy of every person, every car, every crop, every house, every animal, and even every insect and every piece of dirt. You can also activate the Mist for your house, for your car, for your children, and for your pets. Doing it in complete TRUST with the intent of transforming to Unconditional Love & Unconditional Gratitude™ is very different than doing it out of fear (needing to protect). Do you see the difference?

**"I activate my Transformational Mist™
with the intent to infinitely transform all Sources of
everything that it comes in contact with to
Unconditional Love & Unconditional Gratitude™."**

Once you activate your Transformational Mist™, it is active. You do not need to do it every time you fear lower-level energy or when you feel negative energy. Once it's there, it's there. But keep in Mind that if you fear something, you not only attract it, but you activate that energy from within you. That is why it is so important to HEAL fear so you *can* live in complete TRUST.

Don't think it's that easy? What if it is?

Using the Infinite Healing™ tools increases the amount of Unconditional Love & Unconditional Gratitude™ in you, in those around you, in the world, and in the Universe!

Conclusion

You're human. You may not always be happy with the experiences in your life. You'll have thoughts you don't like and don't want. You'll encounter circumstances that trigger anger, disappointment, hurt, and grief. But denying the negative does not mean it is not there, it just means that you're ignoring it. It is still decreasing your overall vibration whether you HONOR it or not.

Living a positive life can be a challenge when you pretend, ignore, or deny that you have negative thoughts and emotions. You cannot TRULY HEAL if you're denying, ignoring, or suppressing anything!

> *Be honest with yourself.*
> *What energy are you*
> *really contributing to the Universe?*

You attract what is on the inside, even if you show the outside world something different. This has a significant impact on what appears in your life. Answer this question truthfully: What thoughts and emotions do you have that are attracting negativity?

> *Don't be afraid of what's on the inside ...*
> *it's the only place you'll find what you need.*

I believe that each and every one of you has the ability to positively impact the world every moment of every day. The most important thing is to HONOR your thoughts and your emotions and to remember to HEAL the less-than-desirable ones. Each time you HEAL the negative in your life, you not only HEAL you, but you HEAL the energy of the world.

"When you HEAL yourself,
everything else just seems to click into place."
—*Testimonial from Jennifer, Infinite Healing*™ *student*

Life is meant to be abundant in everything. Why settle for so little, especially when you now have the tools to TRULY HEAL? Don't think it's that easy? What if it is?

Dare to experience the power of You!

LEARN them, USE them, LIVE them!

Infinite Healing™ Tools

1. HONOR everything about YOURSELF and become aware of the opportunities to HEAL.

2. ACTIVATE ALL LESSONS because if you don't learn the lesson, you *will* get another opportunity.

3. TRANSFORM ALL SOURCES of everything you are feeling or of the situation TO *Unconditional Love & Unconditional Gratitude* ™ because you radiate and attract the same vibration of your energy. You must HEAL the negative in order to increase your frequency and attract more positive things.

The first three tools are the ones for you to use most consistently to achieve the greatest and deepest HEALING. The next three tools are to be used to help you attract what you want in life.

4. NAVIGATE YOUR LIFE and become an active participant in where you want your life to go by activating *all Sources* that create what you want or by setting the *energy the way you want it.*

5. TRUST THAT THE OUTCOME IS OR WILL BE EXACTLY AS IT IS SUPPOSED TO BE because everything you experience in life is either a blessing or an opportunity to learn more Spiritual lessons and to HEAL.

6. BE TRULY GRATEFUL because TRUE GRATITUDE attracts more things to be TRULY GRATEFUL for.

© *Stacie Farnham* ™

www.staciefarnham.com

Infinite Healing™
sees life as a series of OPPORTUNITIES—
opportunities to learn spiritual lessons
and opportunities to HEAL.
Do you take advantage
of the opportunities that
are presented on your Spiritual Course™?

I activate all Sources that create HEALING in YOU!

I TRUST wholeheartedly in the miracle that YOU are. May your life infinitely flow in Unconditional Love & Unconditional Gratitude™.

DIRECTORY OF NEGATIVE EMOTIONS

You can use this list to help you identify what you feel. But remember to not get caught up in trying to define it. Infinite Healing™ works best when you are unfiltered and use your own description of your situation when you transform all Sources.

"I activate all lessons that everyone is to learn from this experience. I transform all Sources of *(insert emotions here)* **and everything else I am feeling to Unconditional Love & Unconditional Gratitude™.**

-A-

Aaaahhhhhh!
Abandoned
Abused
Accused
Addicted
Afraid
Aggravated
Agitated
Alarmed
Alienated
All of this
Alone
Annoyed

Anxious
Apathetic
Apprehensive
Arrogant
Ashamed
At a loss
At fault
At risk
Atrocious
Attacked
Awful
Awkward

-B-

Bad
Baffled
Banned
Banished
Bashful
Beat
Beaten down
Bewildered
Belittled
Berated
Betrayed
Bitterness
Bizarre
Blacklisted
Blackmailed
Blamed
Bleak
Blown away
Blue

Bored
Bossed-around
Bothered
Bothersome
Boxed-in
Broken
Broken down
Broken-hearted
Bruised
Brushed-off
Bugged
Bullied
Bummed
Bummed out
Burdened
Burdensome
Burned
Burned-out

-C-

Captive
Careless
Chaotic
Cheated
Choked
Claustrophobic
Clingy
Closed
Clueless
Clumsy
Coaxed
Coerced
Cold

Cold-hearted
Combative
Competitive
Compulsive
Conceited
Concerned
Compromised
Cast-off
Censored
Chastised
Cheap
Childish
Condemned
Confined
Contradictory
Conflicted
Confronted
Confused
Conned
Constricted
Consumed
Contentious
Controlled by others
Convicted
Cornered
Corralled
Cowardly
Crabby
Cramped
Cranky
Crappy
Crazy
Creeped out
Criticized

Cross
Crippled
Cursed
Crowded
Crummy
Crushed
Cut-down
Cut-off

-D-

Damaged
Damned
Dazed
Deceived
Defamed
Defeated
Defective
Defenseless
Defiant
Deficient
Deflated
Degenerate
Degraded
Dehumanized
Dejected
Demeaned
Demented
Demoralized
Demotivated
Dependent
Depleted
Depraved
Depreciated

Depressed
Deprived
Desecrated
Deserted
Deserving of (lower-level things like pain, punishment, betrayal, etc.)
Desperate
Despicable
Despised
Destitute
Destroyed
Detached
Detestable
Devalued
Devastated
Devoid
Dictated to
Diminished
Dirty
Disabled
Disagreeable
Disappointed in/by
Disappointing
Disapproved of
Disbelieved
Discarded
Disconnected
Discontent
Disconcerted
Discouraged
Discredited
Discriminated
Disempowered
Disenchanted
Disengaged

Disgraced
Disgruntled
Disgusted
Disheartened
Dishonest
Dishonorable
Disillusioned
Disliked
Dismal
Dismayed
Disorganized
Disoriented
Disowned
Displeased
Disposable
Disregarded
Disrespected
Dissatisfied
Distant
Distorted
Distracted
Distrustful
Distraught
Distressed
Disturbed
Dizzy
Dominated
Done
Doomed
Double-crossed
Doubted
Down
Down and out
Down in the dumps

Downcast
Downhearted
Downtrodden
Drained
Dramatic
Dread
Dreary
Dry
Dumb
Dumped
Dumped on
Duped

-E-

Edgy
Egotistical
Elusive
Embarrassed
Emotional
Emotionless
Empty
Endangered
Enraged
Enslaved
Envious
Excluded
Estranged
Entangled
Evaded
Evasive
Evicted
Exasperated
Exhausted

Stacie Farnham

Exploited
Exposed

-F-

Failure
Fake
Fatigued
Fear
Fearful
Fed up
Filthy
Finished
Flawed
Flustered
Forced
Forgetful
Forgettable
Forgotten
Fragile
Fragmented
Frantic
Freaked out
Frightened
Frigid
Frustrated
Furious

-G-

Gloomy
Glum
Greedy
Grey

Grief
Gross
Grossed-out
Grouchy
Grumpy
Guarded
Guilt-tripped
Guilty
Gullible

-H-

Had enough
Harassed
Hard
Hard-hearted
Hassled
Hate
Hateful
Hatred
Haunted
Heartbroken
Heartless
Heavy-hearted
Helpless
Hesitant
Hideous
Hindered
Holding a grudge
Hopelessness
Horrible
Horrified
Hostile
Humiliated

Hung up
Hurried
Hurt
Hushed
Hypocritical
Hysterical

-I-

Idiotic
Ignorant
Ignored
Imbalanced
Immature
Impatient
Imposed-upon
Impotent
Impoverished
Imprisoned
In the dumps
In the way
Inadequate
Incapable
Incompetent
Incompatible
Incomplete
Inconsiderate
Incorrect
Indecisive
Indifferent
Indignant
Ineffective
Inefficient
Inept

Inferior
Inflexible
Infuriated
Inhibited
Insane
Insecure
Insensitive
Insignificant
Insincere
Insufficient
Insulted
Intimidated
Invalidated
Invisible
Irrational
Irresponsible
Irritable
Irritated
Isolated

-J-

Jaded
Jealous
Jerked around
Jittery
Judged
Judgmental
Jumpy
Just going through the motions

-K-

Kept

Stacie Farnham

Kept apart
Kept away
Kept out
Kept quiet

-L-

Lacking
Lacking worthiness
Laughed at
Lazy
Lectured to
Left out
Let down
Lied about
Lied to
Like it's easier to avoid life
Limited
Livid
Lonely
Lonesome
Longing
Lost
Lousy
Loveless
Low

-M-

Mad
Made fun of
Man handled
Manipulated
Materialistic

Mean
Melancholy
Messed with
Messy
Miffed
Minimized
Miserable
Misled
Mistaken
Mistreated
Mistrusted
Misunderstood
Misused
Mixed-up
Mocked
Molested
Mortified

-N-

Nagged
Naughty
Naive
Needing to avoid conflict
Needy
Negative
Neglected
Nervous
Neurotic
Never good enough
Not good enough
Numb

-O-

Obligated
Obnoxious
Obsessed
Obstinate
Offended
On display
On edge
Opinionated
Opposed
Out of control
Out of place
Out of touch
Outraged
Over-controlled
Over-protected
Overlooked
Overwhelmed
Overworked

-P-

Pained
Panicked
Paralyzed
Paranoid
Pathetic
Perplexed
Persecuted
Perturbed
Pessimistic
Petrified
Phony

Picked on
Pissed
Pissed off
Pitiful
Played with
Pooped
Poor
Powerless
Preached to
Preoccupied
Prejudiced
Pressured
Prosecuted
Protected
Provoked
Psychopathic
Psychotic
Pulled apart
Pulled back
Punished
Puny
Pushed
Pushed away
Put down
Puzzled

-Q-

Questioned

-R-

Rage
Raped

Rattled
Regret
Rejected
Remorse
Repulsive
Resented
Resentful
Resentment
Resistant
Responsible
Restless
Restrained
Restricted
Retarded
Revengeful
Ridiculed
Ridiculous
Robbed
Rotten
Ruined
Rushed

-S-

Sad
Sadistic
Safer to hide away
Sarcastic
Scared
Scarred
Scattered
Scorned
Screwed
Screwed over

Screwed up
Seething
Self-centered
Self-conscious
Self-destructive
Self-hatred
Selfish
Shaky
Shallow
Shame
Shocked
Shot down
Shunned
Shy
Sick
Singled-out
Slammed
Slandered
Slighted
Slow
Small
Smothered
Sorrow
Snapped at
Spiteful
Stagnant
Stereotyped
Stifled
Stressed
Stretched
Stubborn
Stuck
Stuffy
Stumped
Stupid

Submissive
Sucked dry
Suffocated
Suicidal
Superficial
Superior
Suppressed
Suspicious

-T-

Taken advantage of
Tense
Terrible
Terrified
Thoughtless
Threatened
Timid
Tired
Tortured
Trapped
Troubled
Tuned out
Turned off

-U-

Unappreciated
Uncertain
Uncomfortable
Undecided
Under nurtured
Underappreciated
Undesirable
Undisciplined

Uneasy
Unfulfilled
Unhappy
Unimportant
Unloved
Unorganized
Unprotected
Unsettled
Unsure
Untrusting
Unwanted
Upset
Uptight
Used
Useless

-V-

Victimized
Violated
Vulnerable
Vengeful

-W-

Wasted
Washed up
Weak
Withdrawn
Worried
Worthless
Wounded
Wrong

Stacie Farnham

List other emotions that you feel here:

_____   _____
_____   _____
_____   _____
_____   _____
_____   _____
_____   _____

What are you afraid of / what do you fear?

_____   _____
_____   _____
_____   _____
_____   _____
_____   _____

"I activate all lessons that everyone is to learn from all
situations in which I feel or have felt fear. I transform
all Sources of fear of *(insert what you're afraid of here)* to
Unconditional Love & Unconditional Gratitude™."

INFINITE HEALING™ PHYSICAL REFERENCE CHART

Remember to *always*
Activate all Lessons you are to learn from the experience(s)
before you **Transform all Sources to UL & UG!**

Physical Disturbance	Emotion(s) triggered from your perception of the situation	Infinite Healing™ Statements "I activate all lessons I am to learn from all of the experiences that create or contribute to the disturbances in my physical Body."
Bacteria	♦ Guilt	"I transform all Sources of guilt and everything else I am feeling to Unconditional Love & Unconditional Gratitude™."

Physical Disturbance	Emotion(s) triggered from your perception of the situation	Infinite Healing™ Statements "I activate all lessons I am to learn from all of the experiences that create or contribute to the disturbances in my physical Body."
Virus	♦ Lack of worthiness ♦ Feeling like you're not good enough	"I transform all Sources of feeling like I'm not good enough and everything else I'm feeling to Unconditional Love & Unconditional Gratitude™."
Fungus	♦ Resentment	"I transform all Sources of resentment and everything else I'm feeling to Unconditional Love & Unconditional Gratitude™."
Parasites	♦ Feeling like you are or have been taken advantage of	"I transform all Sources of feeling like I'm being taken advantage of and everything else I'm feeling to Unconditional Love & Unconditional Gratitude™."

Physical Disturbance	Emotion(s) triggered from your perception of the situation	**Infinite Healing™ Statements** *"I activate all lessons I am to learn from all of the experiences that create or contribute to the disturbances in my physical Body."*
Adrenals	◆ Resentment ◆ Regret ◆ Defeat - no longer caring for oneself ◆ Anxiety ◆ Exhaustion ◆ Trying to please everyone ◆ Fear of things not working out like you want	"I transform all Sources of *(insert emotions here)* and everything else I'm feeling to Unconditional Love & Unconditional Gratitude™."
Bladder	◆ Fear of not being enough *(for someone else or yourself)* ◆ Fear of failure; Fear of letting go of the past ◆ Past hurt ◆ Guilt *(if bacteria is present)* ◆ Lack of courage	"I transform all Sources of *(insert emotions here)* and everything else I'm feeling to Unconditional Love & Unconditional Gratitude™."

Physical Disturbance	Emotion(s) triggered from your perception of the situation	Infinite Healing™ Statements "I activate all lessons I am to learn from all of the experiences that create or contribute to the disturbances in my physical Body."
Colon	● Unwillingness to let go of the past ● Unwillingness or inability to let go of old lower-level emotions like guilt, anger, resentment, fear, shame, etc. ● Hesitation to move forward ● Feeling stuck in the past ● Congestion from the past	"I transform all Sources of (insert emotions here) and everything else I'm feeling to Unconditional Love & Unconditional Gratitude™."
Gallbladder	● Bitterness ● Disappointment ● Hard thoughts ● Feeling as if someone has let you down ● Feeling as if you have let someone down	"I transform all Sources of (insert emotions here) and everything else I'm feeling to Unconditional Love & Unconditional Gratitude™."

Physical Disturbance	Emotion(s) triggered from your perception of the situation	Infinite Healing™ Statements
		"*I activate all lessons I am to learn from all of the experiences that create or contribute to the disturbances in my physical Body.*"
Gray Hair	● Feeling that gray hair naturally comes with age ● Believing that we age as we get older ● Accepting stress as a part of life ● Accepting stress in certain situations (having teen children, job, family)	"I transform all Sources of *(insert emotions here)* and everything else I'm feeling to Unconditional Love & Unconditional Gratitude™."
Heart	● Feeling insecure with self or life ● Resisting self from feeling joy ● Fear of judgment ● Resisting the flow of love to self *and* others ● Living life from the head *knowing* that it is against what the HEART knows is right	"I transform all Sources of *(insert emotions here)* and everything else I'm feeling to Unconditional Love & Unconditional Gratitude™."

Physical Disturbance	Emotion(s) triggered from your perception of the situation	Infinite Healing™ Statements *"I activate all lessons I am to learn from all of the experiences that create or contribute to the disturbances in my physical Body."*
Liver	⬧ Anger ⬧ Frustration ⬧ Irritation ⬧ Annoyance ⬧ Shame ⬧ Guilt ⬧ Hatred / Rage ⬧ Blame ⬧ Judgment	"I transform all Sources of *(insert emotions here)* and everything else I'm feeling to Unconditional Love & Unconditional Gratitude™."
Lungs / Bronchials / Sinuses	⬧ Restricting the freedom to be yourself ⬧ Feeling constricted in life ⬧ Feeling depressed about your life ⬧ Lack of worthiness of living life freely - as YOU ⬧ Sorrow	"I transform all Sources of *(insert emotions here)* and everything else I'm feeling to Unconditional Love & Unconditional Gratitude™."

Physical Disturbance	Emotion(s) triggered from your perception of the situation	Infinite Healing™ Statements "I activate all lessons I am to learn from all of the experiences that create or contribute to the disturbances in my physical Body."
Pancreas	◆ Resisting enjoyment of life - Not allowing self to enjoy life ◆ Believing that life is not meant to be joyful ◆ Fear of defeat - fear of being defeated by life ◆ Feeling unworthy of experiencing joy ◆ Sorrow ◆ Sadness	"I transform all Sources of *(insert emotions here)* and everything else I'm feeling to Unconditional Love & Unconditional Gratitude™."
Spine	◆ Feeling like your support structure is weak or lacking ◆ Feeling like your life is about to crumble	"I transform all Sources of *(insert emotions here)* and everything else I'm feeling to Unconditional Love & Unconditional Gratitude™."
Stomach	◆ Dread ◆ Fear of experiencing the unknown or new things ◆ Hopelessness ◆ Anxiety	"I transform all Sources of *(insert emotions here)* and everything else I'm feeling to Unconditional Love & Unconditional Gratitude™."

Physical Disturbance	Emotion(s) triggered from your perception of the situation	Infinite Healing™ Statements "I activate all lessons I am to learn from all of the experiences that create or contribute to the disturbances in my physical Body."
Thyroid	◊ Feeling of being controlled by others ◊ A feeling of being out of control of self ◊ A <u>want</u> to control but feeling like you can't ◊ Wanting to make sure everything turns out like *you* think it should	"I transform all Sources of *(insert emotions here)* and everything else I'm feeling to Unconditional Love & Unconditional Gratitude™."
Uterus / Prostate	◊ Over-nurturing others ◊ Neglecting self-needs for others ◊ Lack of nurturing flow - inability to nurture ◊ Taking too much responsibility for others' lives *(generally for children or parents)*	"I transform all Sources of *(insert emotions here)* and everything else I'm feeling to Unconditional Love & Unconditional Gratitude™."

Acknowledgements

Infinite Healing™ has been influenced by many people throughout my life, but there are a select few who have made the most significant impact on my Spiritual Course™. I would like to give a special "Thank You" to the following people. I am infinitely GRATEFUL for each and every one of you.

- To my husband, Darin, for his unconditional and unwavering support of everything I believe in, even when he hasn't completely understood what I was doing.
- To my daughter Karissa, who is a continual reminder to me that miracles are everywhere. It took us twelve long months to conceive her, and she is my miracle. It was during my pregnancy with her that I became aware of the beauty that GOD gives us in nature and I awakened to a whole new perspective on life. Karissa, I am so proud of who you are.
- To my daughter Jessica, who has always amazed me with her innate connection to GOD. She has allowed me to understand that we each have our own experiences on our individual Spiritual Course™, that the experiences of others are often quite different from our own, that her experiences are *for* her, that her experiences rarely have anything to do with me, and that that's okay. Jessica, I am so proud of who you are.
- To my mother, Ginger for her continual love, support, and understanding, for always being there to be my sounding

board, and for unconditionally believing in me. She is not only my mother, she is my best friend.

- To my former boss, Gary Hunt, for believing in me and my abilities, for giving me opportunities to learn and grow beyond my job description, and for making me step outside of my comfort zone.

- To my dear friend Steve Solomon, for believing in me, for giving me confidence, and for showing me that I *am* worth believing in. Although we lost touch so many years ago, you are forever in my HEART.

- To my students, many of whom have become cherished friends, for their continued TRUST and support of my PATH.

- To GOD, the Universe, for continuing to nudge me when I wasn't listening, for divinely orchestrating my life to perfection, and for giving me the information contained in this book to share with the world.

- To each and every person who has ever appeared on my Spiritual Course™, for giving me blessings, opportunities to learn lessons, opportunities to HEAL, and opportunities to grow spiritually.

ABOUT THE AUTHOR

Stacie Farnham's journey in the natural health care field began over 20 years ago. Her experience includes iridology, muscle-testing, hands-on-healing, essential oils, herbs, and nutrition. She is the owner and president of All About Health, Inc. which she opened in 2002.

She is the creator of Infinite Healing™ and the Prime Meridian GoldZone™ methods (via the feet, the face, and the back), all of which enhance the amazing, natural HEALING power of the Body. She offers these techniques through her business as both services and workshops.

She believes that each person's Body has an instinctive knowledge of what it needs to HEAL, but there are times when it needs a little assistance. The tag line of her business and a phrase that she wholeheartedly believes in is:

Never underestimate the power
of YOUR body to HEAL!

She knows her PURPOSE in life is to teach others not only how to help themselves HEAL, but also help them understand that they are responsible for their own health.

She and her husband, Darin, live in Meridian, Idaho with their two daughters and black Labrador, Angel.

CONNECT WITH STACIE

For the most updated information on Infinite Healing™, visit:

www.staciefarnham.com

To find out more about her business and the Prime Meridian GoldZone™ techniques, visit:

www.AllAboutHealthWellness.com

You can also connect with Stacie here:

Facebook: *www.facebook.com/InfiniteHealingTM*
www.facebook.com/AllAboutHealthIncorporated
Twitter: *twitter.com/StacieFarnham*
LinkedIn: *www.linkedin.com/StacieFarnham*
Pinterest: *www.pinterest.com/StacieFarnham*
Instagram: *www.instagram.com/StacieFarnham*
Selfgrowth.com: www.selfgrowth.com/experts/stacie_farnham.html

Receive a FREE gift with the purchase of this book!
Visit www.staciefarnham.com/freegift to claim your gift!

TESTIMONIALS

+ *Infinite Healing is one of the most amazing, cutting edge tools a person can use to transform their lives. It focuses on the whole body--comprised of the physical, emotional, mental, and spiritual components from which each and every person is made. You will absolutely be amazed! ~ Debby*

+ *I have attended most of the Infinite Healing workshops and have always felt revitalized after the classes. I took your advice from the Financial Abundance class and every time I saw a Chevrolet Avalanche (or similar), I repeated the "mantra".....
"I quickly and easily attract, obtain and have an abundance of money. I am financially abundant." I suddenly saw Avalanches everywhere. I always had to chuckle when I'd be an in intersection and I'd see several at one time. Then one week....not long after the class things started to click. I found two $35 gift certificates misfiled in my filing cabinet. I happened to look on the unclaimed property website and found that an audit had been done on a property that I sold 24 years ago and they owed me an additional $1000!! And then....after years of looking for additional work (I'm a independent contractor), I got hired on with a brand new company. You can bet that I still say my mantra and set the energy whenever I see those Avalanches driving around town. This week, the new company that I am with got two brand new and very large accounts and I got a promotion! Within the next 3-6 months, my income will more than triple! I've just leased an*

office space....I'm hiring an assistant and I was able to get a job for a friend who has been out of work for over a year. The debt that has been plaguing me for years will be completely paid off within a year and absolutely everything is falling into place. You can be sure that Infinite Healing is now an integral part of my life and now I'll be healing other areas of my life so that I can live the life I was meant to live. Thank you Stacie for all you have done for me and for the benefits you are bringing to our world!!
~ Karen

♦ *It is really difficult to explain how deeply Infinite Healing has blessed my life. I have healed many painful and difficult emotional wounds, healing the source and the perceptions of the pain have allowed freedom and happiness that brings me the greatest joy. The greatest understanding has been in realizing I am enough. I have spent years feeling not enough, comparing myself, and feeling insecure in so many ways. As I learned the words to say and felt the power of transforming all things to UL & UG" I feel happy and whole. I use Infinite Healing everyday for myself and for others. I am so grateful for the tools and the knowledge to truly heal both emotionally and physically. By far the greatest thing I've learned is the relationship between what we think and how it effects our physical body. Our thoughts are powerful and that can be for the good or otherwise and that's our choice, but when you learn to think differently and heal your thoughts...WOW, Miracles happen! ~ Kathy*

♦ *I took the "My Life Vision" class offered by Stacie. She really knows how to impart a wealth of information in a concise and quite fun way. Her wonderful smile and sparkly eyes light up when she can sense her class is "getting it". When I made my 'Life Vision Board', one of the things I wanted was more loving relationships with my family. I specifically defined it on the back of the poster by saying I wanted to do more things with my daughters. They do lots of activities together, and I was feeling empty nest and out of the loop. The very next day after the class, I reviewed*

My Vision Board and hung it up where I could see it. Only 2 hours later, my daughters called and asked if I would want to go to a movie with them! Wow! I was ecstatic! As Stacie says, there is no speed limit for getting what you want or for healing! I am anxious to see how my other aspirations work out! Yay!

P.S. My experience with my daughters was not just a one time nice gesture either. We have had sleepovers, home spa times, and have gone out to eat! I'm loving it! ~ Debby

+ *I have used IH in many areas of my life from my relationship with my husband, children, clients, etc. Most specifically, when I run into challenges with my teenage son and his "know it all" moods, I transform the negative sources into unconditional love & unconditional gratitude walk out of the room, take a deep breath, walk back in and it's amazing...we can actually have a great conversation! ~ Valoree*

+ *We all have journeys in our life we don't know how to approach or overcome. For me I was at a point where I really didn't know what or how I was going to approach my past journeys in my life, I wanted to die. My whole life I just pushed things into a bag I want to call "fear", something I never wanted to dig out and approach again. As an adult I tried being the productive, dedicated wife and mother, friend, coworker and put the fake face on to make others not suspect the dark place I really was at. This caught up with me in my early 30s, and my life just didn't make any sense anymore and I wasn't functioning anymore at a level of good and found myself in a very dark place and really didn't see how I was going to approach let alone overcome these dark journeys in my bag of "fear". I knew not facing this bag of "fear" was going to defeat me if I didn't do something; I still had some if very little faith to realize I still have three kiddos who still needed me and a husband who needed me. I reminded myself they weren't at fault here and how could I put them through a funeral and not understand why or blame them for this. I just knew I couldn't do it alone and on my own, I then was referred to All About Health. Stacie introduced me to Infinite Healing and things have been life altering for me in many ways. Infinite Healing is an understanding of your deepest most vulnerable thoughts of your journey through life, you are approaching and healing what you never thought you could approach and overcome. Infinite Healing to me is the safest way to approach these journeys you are not sure you can. YOU get to choose how far YOU are willing to go with the journey and at what point you need to stop and try again. Plus you are healing these journeys and the deeper you go the more you really find out about yourself and how strong you really are. It is time to heal what you never imagined was even there. ~ Nikky*

♦ *In December 2012 I attended an Infinite Healing class focusing on "My Life Vision". My Vision Board outlined all areas of my life, but I chose to focus on finding and maintaining a loving relationship. Through the Infinite Healing process I worked on healing the obstacles keeping me from having a loving relationship and activating all sources which would help me attract the kind of love I was looking for.*

I put my Vision Board on the wall across from my bed so it was the first thing I saw each morning and the last thing I saw each night. The list which contained the attributes I was looking for in a man was hidden behind the board. In May 2013, quite unexpectedly, I met a wonderful man. It felt like I had known him all my life and we built a strong foundation of friendship which blossomed into the love story of my life. I told Stacie Farnham about him and she asked the question; "Did he have all the attributes I had put on my list?" I had not looked at my list for many months as it was hidden behind my Vision Board, so I went home, took down the board and read the list and yes, he had each and every trait that I was looking for.

Today, we are living the life we have both always hoped to live. I am blissfully happy and am so thankful for Infinite Healing and God, who allowed me to heal the past and have the love I have always dreamed of. ~ Karen

NOTES

NOTES

NOTES

NOTES

NOTES

NOTES

NOTES

Notes

In your life you will encounter only two things: blessings and opportunities to learn lessons. All positive experiences are blessings and all less-than-desirable ones are opportunities to learn lessons. When you have an opportunity to learn a lesson, you also have an opportunity to HEAL.

Taking advantage of the opportunities to learn lessons and to HEAL is the key to creating a life of abundance—in everything.

Infinite Healing™ requires you to HONOR everything about yourself becaus ignoring, denying, or suppressing what you really think and feel does not mea you do not think or feel that way and because ignoring or denying the negativ does not mean it is not there.

Discover how easy it is to learn the lessons you are here to learn and how to Tru HEAL negative thoughts, negative emotions, physical symptoms, and all othe less-than-desirable things in your life. HEALING the negative allows the positiv to flow naturally.

Today is a great day to begin to Truly HEAL and to create a better life! Dare experience the power of YOU!

STACIE FARNHAM is the owner and president All About Health, Inc. and has been involved in the natur health field for over twenty years. Her passion is to he people be proactive with their health. She and her husban Darin, have two daughters and live in Meridian, Idaho.

BALBOA
PRESS
A DIVISION OF HAY HOUSE